SINGAPORE

City Trails

Helen Greathead

RAINBOW CITY

UP ALL NIGHT

HEAD IN THE CLOUDS

GET A PIECE OF THE ACTION

...AND RELAX

SHELTER FROM THE STORM

THE DARK SIDE

CHOOSE YOUR ISLAND

WATER WAY TO GO

BACK TO ITS ROOTS

SHOP TILL YOU DROP

NOT JUST NOODLES

GREAT SHAPES

GO WILD IN THE CITY

SINGAPORE STYLE

CROSSING CONTINENTS

Hi... we're Marco and Amelia and we've created 16 awesome themed trails for you to follow.

The pins on this map mark the starting points, and each trail is packed with secrets, stories and lots of other cool stuff. So whether you are an eco warrior, an adrenaline junkie or a foodie, this book has got something for you!

CONTENTS

PAGE NUMBER

HEAD IN THE CLOUDS

Singapore may be famous for its skyscrapers, but there are plenty of other ways to get up high both in and out of the city. And some surprising things to do up there, too.

START

CENTRAL CATCHMENT NATURE RESERVE

SENTOSA CABLE CAR

WOBBLY WALKWAY

CENTRAL CATCHMENT NATURE RESERVE

Wooden steps lead to a narrow, wobbly bridge suspended up to 25m (82ft) above the forest floor. This is the start of a 250m (273 yard) trail that connects the two highest hills in the Central Catchment Nature Reserve. Visitors need to have a head for heights, because once they're up on the bridge, there's no turning back – it's so narrow, you can only walk single file in one direction! Visitors can see all the layers of the tropical rainforest and often spot macaque monkeys swinging through the trees.

HIGH FLYER

SENTOSA CABLE CAR

An easier way to swing above the trees is on the cable car that sets off from Mount Faber (Singapore's second-highest hill) and zips over the water to Sentosa Island. Couples can eat a romantic dinner for two up here, in a special car decorated with flowers – sweet! It's a popular spot for popping the question.

WALKING IN THE AIR

SILOSO BEACH WALK, SENTOSA

ungee arrived in Singapore in August 2017, and rave people can jump from a very high tower ith a rope attached to their ankles. There's lso a swing 40m (131ft) up from the ground, hich carries up to three people, whizzing them own at over 100kph (62mph)! Or you can opt r a walk along the Skybridge, 47m (154ft) the air. Visitors can even make their way rom the top of the tower back to the ground y walking down the outside of the building!

BUNGEE JUMPS GENERALLY HAPPEN 47M (154FT) UP, BUT THERE'S ALSO A SPECIAL OPTION TO JUMP FROM THE ROOF OF THE TOWER — A FULL 50M (164FT) OFF THE GROUND!

THE NEXT LEVEL

PINNACLE@DUXTON

At 50 storeys high, this is the tallest public housing estate in the world and the only one to have two sky gardens linking all its blocks. The gardens are on the 26th floor (for residents only) and 50th floor (for the public). They connect all seven of the buildings and offer some of the best views in Singapore. While the gardens replace greenery that was lost on the ground and provide escape routes in the event of a fire, they're also great for recreation, with children's play areas, a running track, an outdoor gym for the elderly and chairs for sunbathing.

THE 1,848 APARTMENTS INSIDE THE BLOCKS HAVE WALLS MADE FROM LIGHTWEIGHT CONCRETE THAT CAN BE MOVED, SO TENANTS CAN REARRANGE THEIR FLOORPLAN, NOT JUST THE FURNITURE!

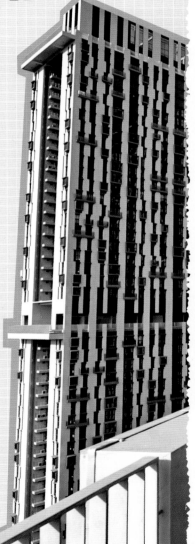

CENTRAL BUSINESS DISTRICT

DOUBLE RUBBLE

Raffles wanted to build Singapore's business centre on a bit of old swampland by the Singapore River. Hundreds of workers flattened a nearby hill and used its rocks and soil to fill in the swamp, raising the level of the surrounding streets. That's how Raffles Place began, and businesses soon moved here, along with Singapore's very first banks and department stores.

REPU
PLA
27
(90

HIGH SOCIETY

CENTRAL BUSINESS DISTRICT

In 1819, when Sir Stamford Raffles bought the island of Singapore from the sultans who ruled it, it was not much more than a village surrounded by jungle and swamps. His plan: to turn the place into a trading post. People came from Europe and all over Asia to settle here and, as the population rose, so did the buildings.

ONE RAFFLES PLACE
278M (911FT)

MINI SINGAPORE

SINGAPORE TAKES ITS CITY PLANNING SERIOUSLY. THE URBAN REDEVELOPMENT AUTHORITY HAS GALLERIES DEVOTED TO THE DEVELOPMENT FROM VILLAGE TO CITY. THE MAIN ATTRACTION IS A 1:400 SCALE MODEL OF THE CENTRAL AREA OF THE CITY. THIS MEANS THE BIGGEST SKYSCRAPERS IN THE CITY ARE JUST 70CM (27IN) TALL. THE BUILDINGS HERE MAY BE SMALL, BUT THIS IS ONE OF THE LARGEST ARCHITECTURAL MODELS IN THE WORLD. IT WAS STARTED DECADES AGO, BUT ITS BUILDINGS ARE ALL BANG UP TO DATE.

CONCRETE CALCULATOR

Like a giant concrete calculator disappearing into the clouds, the OCBC Centre was once the tallest building in Singapore – and the whole of Southeast Asia. Singapore's first major skyscraper was built at warp speed, between 1975 and 1976, but designed to look strong and permanent. It may be almost 100m (328ft) shorter than some of today's shiny new buildings, but it still stands out on the Central Business District (CBD) skyline.

UOB
LAZA ONE
280M
(919FT)

HEAVY CONCRETE
SIDES OUTLINE THE
CALCULATOR SHAPE.

OCBC CENTRE
198M (649FT)

WINDOWS
STICK OUT LIKE
CALCULATOR
BUTTONS.

STRONG LEADERSHIP SKILLS

Lee Kuan Yew (LKY) was Singapore's prime minister for 31 years, and huge changes happened while he was in charge. The island had an important port, but nothing of its own to trade. LKY encouraged new businesses, built new towns with better homes and provided good education. The economy began to boom, and most Singaporeans loved him for it. Some thought LKY went a bit too far, though, in advising people to smile, speak good English and always flush the toilet! He even made spitting illegal and banned the sale of chewing gum!

17%
PERCENTAGE OF SINGAPOREANS
WHO HAVE ASSETS WORTH
US$1 MILLION OR MORE

1967 THE YEAR THE
SINGAPORE
DOLLAR (S$) WAS CREATED

S$10,000
THE BIGGEST SINGAPORE DOLLAR NOTE EVER MADE

HIGH DIVING

MARINA BAY SANDS HOTEL

Some lucky vistors to Singapore can swim in the sky! Well, almost – the swimming pool at this swanky hotel is 200m (656ft) up on top of one of the hotel's towers. It is almost three times the size of an Olympic-sized pool, which makes it the longest roof-top pool in the world.

"What's holding the water in, Dad?"

MARINA BAY SANDS HOTEL

ION SKY OBSERVATORY

A ROOF WITH A VIEW

ION SKY OBSERVATORY

If Singaporeans ever get tired of shopping on Orchard Road, they can just whizz up 55 floors to escape from it all. The ION Sky Observatory doesn't just offer a 360-degree view of the island, visitors can also see all the way to Malaysia! There's a high-tech telescope up here, too, which means whatever the weather, there'll always be a view.

search: MARINA BAY SANDS HOTEL

3,900
The number of people who can visit SkyPark at one time

4,000
The number of beach towels used at SkyPark each day

2,500+
The number of rooms and suites in the hotel

650
The number of plant species in SkyPark

LANE SPOTTING

HANGI AIRPORT

ere's so much to do at Changi, passengers might prefer
aying on the ground to being in the air. As well as shops
d restaurants, there's a butterfly garden, a fish pond,
slide that's 12m (39ft) high and a free 24-hour cinema.
ane-spotters can even watch take-offs and landings from
e luxury rooftop pool. In 2019, Singapore's largest indoor
rden will open here, with the world's tallest indoor waterfall
rain vortex). No wonder it's won the World's Best Airport
ward five years on the trot!

AVIATION PARK ROAD

FIFTY FIFTY

AVIATION PARK ROAD

This location close to the airport is the perfect place to watch
Singapore's air displays. Crowds on the ground gasped during
2015's National Day Parade when 20 aircraft flew across the sky
and formed a number 50! The fly-past marked the death of Lee Kuan
Yew and 50 years of Singaporean independence. It was a tricky
manoeuvre for the Republic of Singapore Air Force pilots: they had
to fly roughly two wingspans apart while maintaining a steady speed
of 600kph (373mph). Yikes!

Whether people prefer to take it fast or slow, there's no shortage of sporting action in Singapore. From scary boat races to calm kite flying, this trail highlights something for everyone.

HIGH KICKING

BEDOK SPORTS CENTRE

The National Schools Championships happen here in Bedok where, among other things, pupils battle it out to become *sepak takraw* champs. *Takraw* is a bit like volleyball, except players can use anything but their hands or arms. Two teams of three try to kick the small woven ball over a net, scoring points if it hits the ground on the other side. It's a fast-paced game, with experienced players leaping in the air, twisting and scissor-kicking the ball then, hopefully, landing safely on their feet!

START

BEDOK SPORTS CENTRE

ON THEIR BIKES

EAST COAST PARK

This park is great for rollerblading, skateboarding, swimming and kayaking, but stretching 15km (9 miles) along the coastline, it's also perfect for cycling. Singapore's main roads can be dangerous for cyclists, but the government is encouraging locals to lower their carbon footprint and get on their bikes. By 2030, they plan to have 700km (435 miles) of cycle paths o the island – that's more than three times the length of Singapore's coastline!

EAST COAST PARK

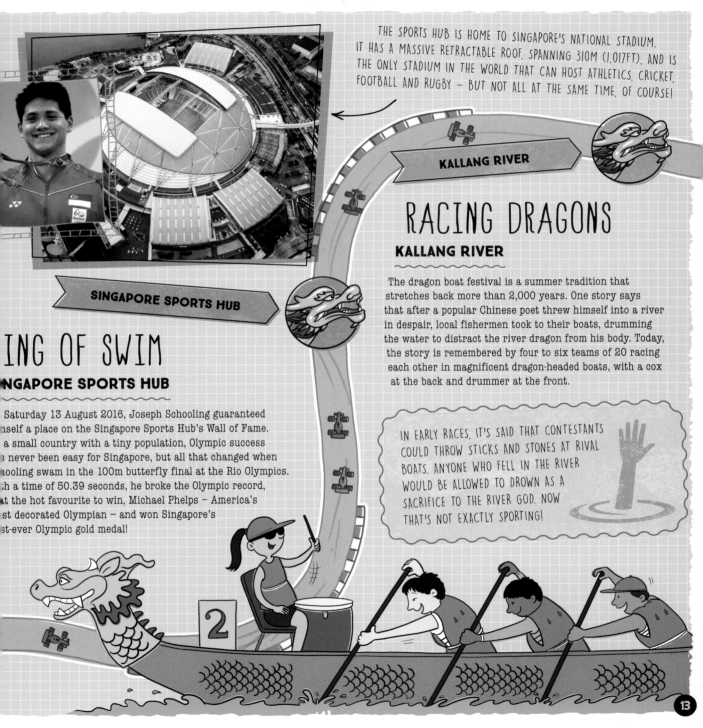

THE SPORTS HUB IS HOME TO SINGAPORE'S NATIONAL STADIUM. IT HAS A MASSIVE RETRACTABLE ROOF, SPANNING 310M (1,017FT), AND IS THE ONLY STADIUM IN THE WORLD THAT CAN HOST ATHLETICS, CRICKET, FOOTBALL AND RUGBY – BUT NOT ALL AT THE SAME TIME, OF COURSE!

KALLANG RIVER

SINGAPORE SPORTS HUB

RACING DRAGONS

KALLANG RIVER

The dragon boat festival is a summer tradition that stretches back more than 2,000 years. One story says that after a popular Chinese poet threw himself into a river in despair, local fishermen took to their boats, drumming the water to distract the river dragon from his body. Today, the story is remembered by four to six teams of 20 racing each other in magnificent dragon-headed boats, with a cox at the back and drummer at the front.

IN EARLY RACES, IT'S SAID THAT CONTESTANTS COULD THROW STICKS AND STONES AT RIVAL BOATS. ANYONE WHO FELL IN THE RIVER WOULD BE ALLOWED TO DROWN AS A SACRIFICE TO THE RIVER GOD. NOW THAT'S NOT EXACTLY SPORTING!

ING OF SWIM

NGAPORE SPORTS HUB

Saturday 13 August 2016, Joseph Schooling guaranteed nself a place on the Singapore Sports Hub's Wall of Fame. a small country with a tiny population, Olympic success s never been easy for Singapore, but all that changed when hooling swam in the 100m butterfly final at the Rio Olympics. h a time of 50.39 seconds, he broke the Olympic record, t the hot favourite to win, Michael Phelps – America's st decorated Olympian – and won Singapore's st-ever Olympic gold medal!

LET'S GO FLY A KITE
MARINA BARRAGE

Marina Barrage can get crowded at weekends, with locals jostling to buy and fly kites. At the Barrage Cove kite shop, kites are tested for fly-ability, and customers can ask advice on which ones suit which conditions. There's even a kite-flying festival here in July each year, with kite-making workshops, stunt-kite performances and a chaotic mix of kite shapes, from large orange centipedes to not very angelic-looking angels. Kids love Lolli-Drop, when over 100 mini parachutes float to the ground. They can rest their aching arms and chomp on a parachute's cargo of free sweets.

4KG (9LB)
WEIGHT A DRIVER
SWEATS OFF
IN ONE RACE

780 MILLION
VIEWERS
WORLDWIDE

ZOOMTOWN
MARINA BAY STREET CIRCUIT

The manhole covers are welded shut, 1,500 lighting projectors illuminate the course and there's a rumbling in the air... Singapore has been a Formula One city since 2008 and its Grand Prix track zooms past some of the most spectacular sights – not that the drivers get to look! The course is tough, and even though these are night-time races, heat is always an issue. The 5km (3 mile) track has a whopping 23 corners, so overtaking is tricky and sparks fly, which means there are fireworks during the race as well as after!

MARINA BARAGE

14

search: SINGAPORE WALKERS

STREET CHAMPS

Walking the city streets may not be a sport (yet) but the people of Singapore are the fastest pedestrians on the planet. On average, they rush around town at 6kph (3.7mph)!

THE BOTANIC GARDENS

YOU CAN FLY!

SENTOSA

With a bit of training, anyone aged seven or over can try to fly at iFly! You just slip on the goggles, suit and helmet and step into the cold, blowy wind tunnel. First-timers start by 'belly-flying' – balancing on the air with bellies flat, arms out, chin up and legs like a frog – and it's not easy! With a bit of concentration, though, you'll manage to take in the view, because transparent tunnel walls mean, just like on a real skydive, fliers can see out over the South China Sea.

iFly's indoor skydiving team holds no less than ten Guinness World Records, including:

- **the most skydivers in a wind tunnel = 13**

- **the most forward rolls in a wind tunnel in a minute = 68**

- **the most passes through a hula hoop in a wind tunnel in a minute = 57**

GOING SLOWWW

THE BOTANIC GARDENS

Soon after the Botanic Gardens open at 5am, locals can be seen moving in slow motion on the grass – some even do it with a ceremonial sword! Tai chi is a bit like meditation with movement. It doesn't look like strenuous exercise, but then it's not just about the body, it's about the mind as well. Older Chinese people believe tai chi will prolong their lives, but it's good for children, too, helping their concentration and calming their mood.

BACK TO ITS ROOTS

According to legend, Singapore got its name back in the 14th century, when a visiting Indonesian prince spied what he thought was a lion. Thinking that this was a good sign, he decided to found a city, which he called Singapura, on the very same spot. In Sanskrit, *simha* and *pura* mean 'lion' and 'city'. Singapura exchanged goods with Chinese, Arab and Portuguese traders, but it wasn't much more than a small fishing village when along came Sir Stamford Raffles...

POPULATION OF SINGAPORE
5.5 MILLION

900% INCREASE IN 5 YEARS
BETWEEN 1819 AND 1824 SINGAPORE'S POPULATION WENT FROM 1,000 TO 10,000

START

RAFFLES LANDING

OLD PARLIAMENT HOUSE

A MAN WITH A MISSION

RAFFLES LANDING

Raffles arrived on the island early in 1819, looking for a way to improve British trade in Southeast Asia. Before long, he'd signed a treaty, hoisted the British flag and started making big changes. Raffles Landing marks his arrival point with a statue. Even though Raffles and British rule are long gone, the statue is still seen as a symbol of Singapore — it's a popular selfie spot too.

PAP IN PARLIAMENT

OLD PARLIAMENT HOUSE

Nowadays, Singaporeans call it the Arts House, but this building was completed in 1827 as part of Raffles' town plan, and it's one of the oldest colonial buildings in Singapore. It became known as Parliament House in 1959, after the People's Action Party (PAP), led by Lee Kuan Yew (LKY), won the right to govern Singapore.

FAREWELL LKY

NEW PARLIAMENT HOUSE

LKY took up residence in these smart new government buildings in 1999. He devoted his life to Singapore and when he died in 2015, 415,000 people came to New Parliament House to visit his coffin. Overall, 1.2 million mourners paid their respects to their former prime minister. Some queued for nearly ~~~en hours, and the weather was so hot that lots of people fainted ~~d had to be carried off on stretchers!

MOURNERS RECEIVING MEDICAL TREATMENT IN SINGAPORE SUMMER HEAT

48-YEARS' HARD LABOUR

ST. ANDREW'S CATHEDRAL

Between 1825 and 1873, convicts from India were transported to Singapore. The city was growing fast, and labour was in short supply, so the convicts were quickly put to work clearing swamps, building roads, bridges and huge structures like this one, which took 12 years to complete.

THE CATHEDRAL'S WHITE WALLS ARE SMOOTH AND SHINY THANKS TO A PLASTER MADE OF EGG WHITE, SUGAR, WATER AND COCONUT HUSKS, WHICH WAS POLISHED WITH ROCK CRYSTALS AND DUSTED WITH SOAPSTONE POWDER. NO WONDER IT TOOK AGES TO FINISH!

STILL STANDING

PADANG AREA

Slap bang in the middle of Singapore, you will find an old playing field lined with colonial buildings. The Old City Hall and Supreme Court were once separate buildings, but today they're connected and have become the National Gallery Singapore. If these old buildings could talk, they'd have an awful lot to say...

SMASHING TIME

The Supreme Court officially opened in 1939. With its ornate pillars and dome, it was designed to look like London's Old Bailey courthouse. The building has an eight-sided foundation stone set into the entrance floor. It hides a time capsule containing Singapore newspapers and coins, all dated 1937. The architect obviously thought the building would stand the test of time, because the stone is not to be smashed until 3000!

BESIDE THE SEA

The old City Hall was completed in 1929. Its fancy front, with 18 huge concrete columns and a grand staircase, was intended to show off the might of the British Empire to ships approaching the harbour. Back then, everyone and everything arrived by boat, and only the Padang separated City Hall and the seafront. Today, the building hasn't shifted an inch, but thanks to land reclamation, there's a whole new waterfront over at Marina Bay.

OLD SUPREME COURT
BUILT 1937–1939

NATIONAL GALLERY SINGAPORE
OPENED 2015

HISTORY HAPPENS AT THE HALL

City Hall has a rather dramatic past...

1941 Japanese bombs started falling and locals sheltered here.

1942 The Japanese invaded and took City Hall for themselves, rounding up Allied prisoners of war in front of the building and marching them all the way to Changi POW camp, where they would be imprisoned... or worse.

1945 After four long years of occupation, the Japanese finally surrendered to the British inside the City Hall Chamber. Meanwhile, outside, crowds gathered on the Padang, ready to march again – this time in a victory parade.

1959 The right-wing People's Action Party won their first election, and Lee Kuan Yew was sworn in here as Singapore's first elected prime minister.

1963 LKY stood on the steps of City Hall to announce that British rule had ended and Singapore would now become a state with Malaysia.

1965 LKY cried when he was forced to announce that the alliance with Malaysia had not worked out. Instead, Singapore became a republic and the prime minister's office was moved to City Hall.

A GOOD GOSSIP

BACK IN 1819, RAFFLES WANTED THE LARGE OPEN AREA, NOW CALLED THE PADANG, TO BE A PLAYGROUND FOR ALL SINGAPOREANS. CRICKET, TENNIS, RUGBY AND HOCKEY MATCHES HAVE ALL BEEN PLAYED ON THE GRASS OVER THE YEARS, AND THERE ARE STILL TWO CRICKET CLUBS HERE. THE HILL IN ONE CORNER WAS USED FOR A DIFFERENT KIND OF 'PLAY'. IT'S WHERE EUROPEANS USED TO GO FOR A GOOD GOSSIP AND IT'S STILL KNOWN AS 'SCANDAL POINT' TODAY.

NEW SUPREME COURT
OPENED 2005

OLD CITY HALL
BUILT 1926–1929

NATIONAL GALLERY SINGAPORE

BLOW AWAY THE STONE
NATIONAL MUSEUM OF SINGAPORE

In 1819, an enormous stone was discovered by the Singapore River. Crowds of people of all nationalities came to see it, fascinated by the 50 lines of writing inscribed on its surface. Then, in 1843 impatient builders blew up the stone so that they could widen the river, and only a few pieces were rescued and shipped off to museums. The one piece left in Singapore is inside this museum. Experts think the writing on the stone holds the secrets of Singapore's past – if only they could work out what it said!

RAFFLES HOTEL

NATIONAL MUSEUM OF SINGAPORE

GET YOUR SKATES ON

RAFFLES HOTEL

Raffles was long dead by 1887, when a 10-room hotel was opened in his name. The next year, a couple of literary legends visited the hotel and its reputation began to spread. The hotel has added some lavish extensions over the years. When a new building opened in 1899, boasting Singapore's first electric lights and fans – and even a French chef – visitors flocked from around the world. There were parties and dinner dances six nights of the week, including 'skating dinners' where guests waltzed about the enormous ballroom on roller skates.

search: RAFFLES FACTS

○ ANIMAL HOTEL

In 1902, an escaped circus tiger called Stripes found its way under the hotel billiard room. Help was summoned from a Mr Philips, who arrived in his pyjamas and shot the poor beast. It was the last tiger ever killed in Singapore.

60,000
NUMBER OF ORCHIDS ON DISPLAY

THE WORLD'S LARGEST ORCHID IS THE TIGER ORCHID, WHICH ONCE GREW WILD IN SINGAPORE AND HAS NOW BEEN REINTRODUCED. A LARGE CLUMP OF THESE FLOWERS CAN WEIGH UP TO A TONNE!

RCHIDS GALORE
NGAPORE BOTANIC GARDENS

ngapore's national flower is an orchid. This and many
er types of flower have been grown in the Botanic
rdens since the 1870s, and experiments with new
rieties began in the 1920s. Today, the National Orchid
rden houses the largest display of orchids in Asia.
w species created here are named after VIPs who have
ited, including Nelson Mandela, Jackie Chan, and the
ke and Duchess of Cambridge, and are all on display
the VIP Orchid Garden.

A NASTY SURPRISE
FORMER FORD FACTORY

During the Second World War, Singapore was still
a British colony. The British expected an attack
from the sea, but Japanese troops travelled down
through Malaysia on bicycles. They snuck onto
the island across a narrow stretch of water and
attacked. The Allies fought back for a week, but
when they ran out of ammunition, the Japanese
quickly took charge. Turning the Ford Factory
into their headquarters, they were soon using
it to churn out Nissan army trucks.

THE BRITISH OFFICIALLY SURRENDERED TO THE JAPANESE IN THE BOARD ROOM HERE. TODAY, THE FRONT OF THE FACTORY IS A WWII MUSEUM, WHERE, SADLY, THE BOARD ROOM IS BETTER KNOWN AS THE SURRENDER ROOM.

FORMER FORD FACTORY

SHOP TILL YOU DROP

Singapore is one of the richest places in the world, with millionaires living in one out of every ten households! So it's hardly a surprise that the city is one of the world's most expensive. While it's easy to find cheap eats and drinks, locals pay a fortune to own a car and buy clothes. Not that the price tag stops most Singaporeans – they absolutely love to shop.

A GEM OF A SHOP

LOUIS VUITTON

One shop with bags of millionaire appeal is Louis Vuitton (LV). Built to float on its own little island, it stands out of the bay like a giant cut gemstone. Inside, it's designed to look like a very posh yacht, with teak floors, rope handles and even portholes. The glass walls are screened to protect shoppers – and LV's luxury leather bags – from the effects of the sun. Those who can afford a S$4,400 (£2,500) handbag will probably be welcome in the VIP lounge, too.

VIP

WHAT'S UP DOC?

EU SANG TCM CLINIC

Traditional Chinese Medicine (TCM) is popular in Singapore, this little shop stocks essential ingredients such as black fu eucommia bark and ginseng. Visitors need a consultation be they can buy, and TCM physicians have interesting examina techniques. As well as listening to the lungs and taking the voice and take a look at the colour of their tongue!

START

LOUIS VUITTON ISLAND

EU SANG TCM CLINIC

EARLY TO MARKET

CHINATOWN COMPLEX

Locals find the freshest foods at wet markets, which actually have a wet and dry side. The wet side sells meat and fish (it's wet from regular floor washings), while the dry side sells products such as beans, spices and noodles. Chinatown's market has vegetables on one side and live lobsters, eels and frogs on the other. For extra-fresh food, shoppers arrive early — the market opens at four in the morning! After ticking everything off the shopping list, they might stop for a refreshing breakfast of... er... frog porridge!

WORTH WAITING FOR

LIM CHEE GUAN

Co-workers take turns to wait patiently in the very long line outside Lim Chee Guan. They know that when they get to the front, their *bak kwa* will be one of the best in Singapore. *Bak kwa* is a speciality of Chinese New Year, traditionally made from sliced pork that's air-dried and then cooked over hot charcoal. Sweet, savoury and smoky all at the same time, *bak kwa* comes in other flavours, too, such as chicken or chilli. There's even a vegetarian version and one made with pineapple!

LIM CHEE GUAN

23

"I'll only be a minute dear ..."

FASHION FRUIT
ORCHARD ROAD

Orchard Road gets its name from the fruit trees that grew here in the 19th century. The area was home to nutmeg and pepper farms too. Singapore's first supermarket opened here over 100 years ago and today, the road isn't lined with shops, it's lined with shopping centres, each with loads of shops inside! From high street brands to top design houses, Asian art to tattoo parlours, it's a shopper's paradise and one of the most famous shopping streets in Asia.

FROM TOMB TO BOOM
TANGS, ORCHARD ROAD

When C. K. Tang expanded his shop selling Chinese handicrafts onto a patch of land opposite a cemetery, people thought he'd lost his marbles. But the site was on the route between home and work for many people who had come to Singapore from other countries. Tangs began importing goods to appeal to them, and before long, business was really booming. Soon, other stores opened, and Orchard Road really took off. Tang Plaza is now a 33-storey shopping and hotel complex, topped off in true Chinese style with a pointy, pagoda-shaped roof.

SINGAPORE'S FIRST-EVER TATTOO ARTIST, JOHNNY TWO THUMBS, MADE A NAME FOR HIMSELF TATTOOING AMERICAN SAILORS DURING WWII. TWO GENERATIONS ON, HIS GRANDDAUGHTER, SUTATTOO, IS CARRYING ON THE FAMILY TRADITION. HER TATTOOS ARE CONSIDERED SOME OF THE BEST IN THE CITY, EVEN THOUGH SU HERSELF HAS CHOSEN NOT TO HAVE A SINGLE TATTOO.

lonely planet

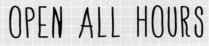

HEERY AND CHEAP

JGIS STREET MARKET

stomers don't need to bring a weighty wallet when they come
Singapore's biggest market, because it's cheap and very
eerful! More than 800 shops stay open until 10 or 11pm,
ling all sorts of items, from quirky teen fashion to sunglasses,
ellery and funny souvenirs. And Singapore's shoppers never
hungry – there are loads of juice bars serving brightly coloured
nks and plenty of places to snack – octopus balls anyone?

OPEN ALL HOURS

MUSTAFA CENTRE

Today, Ahmed Mustaq is one of Singapore's richest
residents, so it's hard to believe that as a boy he worked
14 hours a day selling his wares on the streets of
Singapore. He moved here from India with his dad,
Mustafa, and in 1971, the two of them opened a clothes
shop. Their business grew slowly and steadily, and today,
Mustafa's offers six levels of shopping heaven that
are open 24/7. The store sells just about everything,
especially if it's Indian – dazzling saris, scarily hot ghost
chillis, bling-tastic jewellery and even... cow's urine!

ACCORDING TO THE HINDU RELIGION, THE COW
IS SACRED, SO ITS PEE IS THOUGHT TO BE
PRETTY SPECIAL. *GAU JAL*, OR COW WATER,
IS USED IN RELIGIOUS CEREMONIES, BUT SOME
PEOPLE BELIEVE THEY CAN PROTECT THEIR
BODIES AGAINST DISEASE – BY DRINKING IT!

search: SPENDING HABITS

Each month, young families spend around:

14% OF THEIR INCOME IN HAWKER CENTRES
(FOOD MARKETS)
10% ON LEISURE ACTIVITIES
5% ON COMMUNICATION
3% ON CLOTHING AND SHOES

GREAT SHAPES

From a loaf of bread balanced on top of three towers, to a fruity theatre and a chopstick-like memorial, this trail follows some of the weirdest and most wonderful structures that shape Singapore's skyline.

START

MARINA BAY SANDS HOTEL

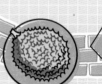

ARTSCIENCE MUSEUM

A HANDY IDEA
ARTSCIENCE MUSEUM

This amazing museum looks like a lotu[s] flower floating on a pond, or a ten-finge[r] hand. The intention is to catch enough rainwater in the huge bowl-shaped pal[m] or roof, to feed a waterfall in the centr[e of] the building – and the loos, too! Skyligh[ts] in each of the building's fingers let nat[ural] light flood into the upper galleries, whi[le] air-conditioning grills in the floor save[s] energy by only cooling the space up to visitor height.

BOAT OR BAGUETTE?
MARINA BAY SANDS HOTEL

Architect Moshe Safdie based his design for the towers of the Marina Bay Sands Hotel on the shape of a deck of cards. But is that a boat or half a baguette that's balancing on top? Actually, it's the hotel's own sky park, complete with swimming pool (see page 10). The park is so big it could accommodate three of the world's largest passenger planes! As well as its famous infinity pool, restaurants, cafés and an observation deck, it is home to over 650 species of plants.

50.8CM

The distance special joints und[er] the swimming pool can move to keep the pool water level

500

Number of stabilising jacks that a[re] needed to stop pool water from sp[illing] down onto the city streets below

A MOVING EXPERIENCE

SINGAPORE FLYER

For a while, this Ferris wheel was the largest in the world after it opened in 2008, and it is still one of Asia's most popular attractions. It provides stunning views of the city, and riding all the way round is an amazing experience when the lights come on at night. But most spectacular of all, on a clear day, the views from the top stretch up to 48km (30 miles), as far as neighbouring Malaysia and even Indonesia!

"I can see for miles and miles and..."

HE APPLIANCE OF SCIENCE

HE HELIX

el spirals within steel spirals create a double helix – the shape of DNA that's nd in all living organisms – so pedestrians walk through this bridge rather than r it. The structure might look complicated, but its shape is actually economical. h the help of clever science, the design uses far less steel than other types of dge, and it's a special sort of steel that doesn't need constant maintenance. e inside spirals shield pedestrians from the heat of the sun, built-in viewing tforms show off awesome views, and then at night the whole bridge lights up!

THEATRE BY THE WATER

THE ESPLANADE

When the Esplanade Theatres first opened in 2002, Singaporeans weren't all that impressed and they came up with some pretty unflattering nicknames for the two strange-shaped domes that rose up by the river. Marshmallows, fish scales and bug's eyes were among them. Eventually, though, one name came out on top: the durian.

DURIAN (AKA STINKY FRUIT!)

THE ESPLANADE

OUT
THE

SHOPPING MALL

3,000 PERFORMANCES EACH YEAR

26+ MILLION
SPECTATORS SINCE ITS OPENING

S$600 MILLION
THE TOTAL COST OF CREATING THE ESPLANADE BUILDINGS

1,950-SEAT THEATRE

STRANGE FRUIT

SINGAPOREANS CALL THE DURIAN THE KING OF FRUITS BECAUSE IT'S SO BIG AND SO SPIKEY. UNFORTUNATELY, DURIANS ALSO SMELL SO BAD THAT THEY'RE BANNED ON PUBLIC TRANSPORT (SPECIAL SIGNS GET THE MESSAGE ACROSS). DESPITE THE SMELL — SOMETHING LIKE ROTTING FLESH MIXED WITH RUBBISH — THE FRUIT IS SWEET AND CUSTARDY INSIDE WITH HINTS OF BANANA AND ALMOND. SOME PEOPLE JUST CAN'T GET ENOUGH OF IT, SO THE NAME IS KIND OF A COMPLIMENT.

PIKE-TACULAR

The Esplanade buildings weren't designed to look like anything in particular. The two domes are lightweight covers for the two main performance spaces, and the spikes are actually triangular windows with pointy aluminium sunshades. They're designed to open and close to stop the glare and heat of the sun, without messing up the view. Natural light filters in during the day, and at night the domes light up like spike-tacular lanterns.

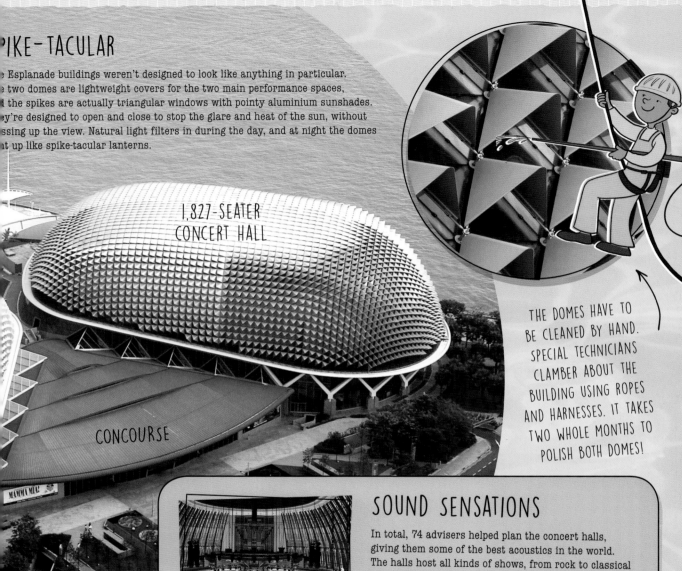

1,827-SEATER
CONCERT HALL

CONCOURSE

THE DOMES HAVE TO BE CLEANED BY HAND. SPECIAL TECHNICIANS CLAMBER ABOUT THE BUILDING USING ROPES AND HARNESSES. IT TAKES TWO WHOLE MONTHS TO POLISH BOTH DOMES!

SOUND SENSATIONS

In total, 74 advisers helped plan the concert halls, giving them some of the best acoustics in the world. The halls host all kinds of shows, from rock to classical to gamelan (traditional Indonesian music), and the acoustics can be tailored to suit each one. Special banners are adjusted, canopies raised and lowered, and 58 concrete doors connecting to a reverberation hall can be opened and closed as necessary. For shows with lots of performers – such as Chinese opera or Indian dance – the stage is widened from 14m (46ft) to 16.5m (54ft)!

NEVER FORGET

THE CIVILIAN WAR MEMORIAL

~

War memorials are usually dedicated to soldiers, but this structure honours the thousands of ordinary Singaporeans who were killed after the Japanese invaded and occupied Singapore in 1942. Mass graves were unearthed around the island in the 1960s, and the remains were reburied under this monument, never to be forgotten. Its four tall pillars represent Malay, Chinese, Indian and Eurasian people killed during the occupation. Locals affectionately call this monument 'the chopsticks' because of its shape.

THE CIVILIAN WAR MEMORIAL

EACH CHOPSTICK IS

68M (23 FT) HIGH

50,000

NUMBER OF CIVILIANS KILLED BETWEEN **1942 & 1945**

HENDERSON WAVES

WAVE TO THE BIRDS

HENDERSON WAVES

~

Walkers come across this beautiful structure close to the start of the 10km (6 miles) Southern Ridges Trail. When people are 36m (118ft) up, they hardly notice the busy road down below as they stroll across the wood-lined bridge that connects one lush green space to another. Steel ribs weave up and down seven times to create the shape of the wave, providing shelter from the sun or rain. This is the perfect place to get up close and personal with a raptor or two.

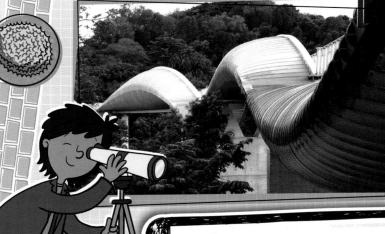

search: ISLAND SHAPES

Singapore's 63 islands have some interesting natural shapes, too:

SINGAPORE'S MAIN ISLAND = a diamond
SENTOSA = an ice-cream cone
UBIN = a sock
JURONG = a flying bird
TEKONG = a person drinking a cup of tea

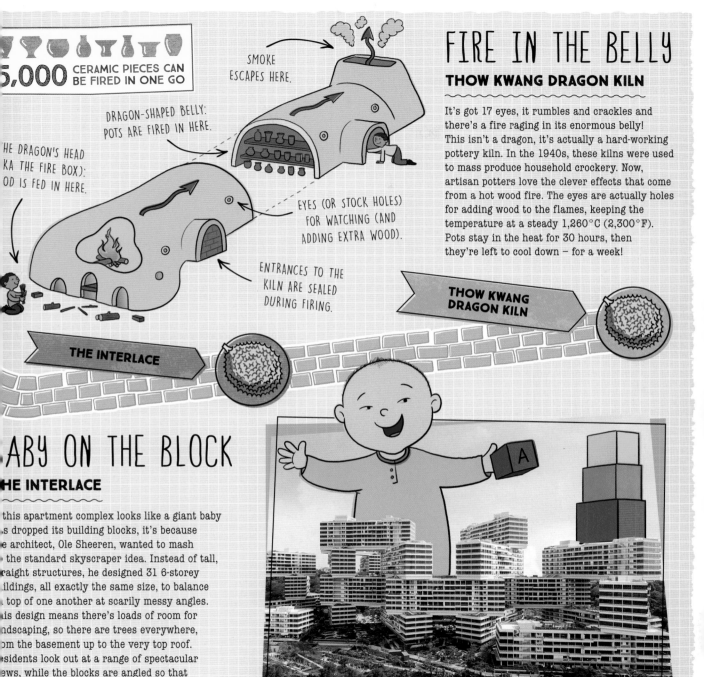

5,000 CERAMIC PIECES CAN BE FIRED IN ONE GO

SMOKE ESCAPES HERE.

DRAGON-SHAPED BELLY: POTS ARE FIRED IN HERE.

THE DRAGON'S HEAD (AKA THE FIRE BOX): WOOD IS FED IN HERE.

EYES (OR STOCK HOLES) FOR WATCHING (AND ADDING EXTRA WOOD).

ENTRANCES TO THE KILN ARE SEALED DURING FIRING.

FIRE IN THE BELLY
THOW KWANG DRAGON KILN

It's got 17 eyes, it rumbles and crackles and there's a fire raging in its enormous belly! This isn't a dragon, it's actually a hard-working pottery kiln. In the 1940s, these kilns were used to mass produce household crockery. Now, artisan potters love the clever effects that come from a hot wood fire. The eyes are actually holes for adding wood to the flames, keeping the temperature at a steady 1,260°C (2,300°F). Pots stay in the heat for 30 hours, then they're left to cool down – for a week!

THOW KWANG DRAGON KILN

THE INTERLACE

BABY ON THE BLOCK
THE INTERLACE

If this apartment complex looks like a giant baby has dropped its building blocks, it's because the architect, Ole Sheeren, wanted to mash up the standard skyscraper idea. Instead of tall, straight structures, he designed 31 6-storey buildings, all exactly the same size, to balance on top of one another at scarily messy angles. This design means there's loads of room for landscaping, so there are trees everywhere, from the basement up to the very top roof. Residents look out at a range of spectacular views, while the blocks are angled so that nosy neighbours can't see in.

CROSSING CONTINENTS

Singapore's population is made up of so many different nationalities, taking a stroll across the city can feel a bit like walking across countries, or even continents!

BLUE BUILDING

BABA HOUSE

The brilliant-blue Baba House is a 100-year-old Peranakan building that was once home to shipping tycoon, Wee Bin. It's been lavishly restored outside and inside, too, where there are intricate wood carvings on the walls, elaborately framed Wee Bin family portraits, and fancy items of furniture – including a fabulously colourful marriage bed that's decorated with golden bats for good luck!

IN THE PERANAKAN CULTURE, 'BABA' MEANS MAN, AND 'NYONYA' MEANS WOMAN.

THE REAL LOCALS

The word *peranakan* means 'local' and it's generally used to describe Chinese people who were born in Singapore – though there are Indian and Arab Peranakan, too. Some can trace their ancestors back to the 15th-century traders who left their homelands behind to move here and married native Singaporeans.

LADDER CAKES ARE FOR PROSPERITY.

SPECIAL MOULDS ARE USED FOR MAKING PERANAKAN CAKES AND PASTRIES.

WOBBLY CAKES

Peranakan cuisine is also called Nyonya food because, traditionally, Peranakan girls had to be able to cook if they wanted to marry well. It's a mixture of Chinese and Malaysian cooking styles, with a dash of European thrown in. Colourful Peranakan puddings are available on some hawker (food vendor) stalls. The stripey ladder cake is made from rice flour, sago (see page 61), coconut, beans, syrup, eggs and pandan leaves. It's got a unique wobbly texture, and people tend to love it, or hate it!

BRIGHT WEDDING

Traditional Peranakan weddings were fancy affairs, lasting 12 days! There was special furniture, swanky gifts and a beautiful outfit for the bride. The Peranakan Museum displays 100-year-old wedding garments made from silk and cotton imported from China and stitched with golden thread. Decorated with peonies and butterflies for good luck, they are a blinding shocking pink!

TO KEEP THE PLACE COOL, IT'S DELIBERATELY DARK INSIDE, AND THE STAIRWELL IS ACTUALLY AN 'AIRWELL', ITS ROOF OPEN TO THE ELEMENTS.

UNHAPPY ENDINGS

INTEREST IN THE PERANAKAN CULTURE HAS GROWN SINCE THE 34 EPISODES OF *THE LITTLE NYONYA* AIRED ON TV IN 2008. IT COVERED 70 YEARS OF 20TH-CENTURY PERANAKAN HISTORY AND WAS SINGAPORE'S MOST VIEWED DRAMA SERIES IN 15 YEARS. BY THE TIME OF THE FINAL EPISODE, ONE IN THREE SINGAPOREANS WAS HOOKED. SO MANY OF THEM WERE DISAPPOINTED BY THE UNHAPPY ENDING THAT THE WRITER LATER OFFERED UP FIVE ALTERNATIVE VERSIONS AND ASKED VIEWERS TO VOTE FOR THEIR FAVOURITE.

NOT A BON VOYAGE

TELOK AYER STREET

Immigrants endured perilous journeys to get to Singapore, often escaping from war, poverty and starvation. Then their first year would be spent in hard labour to pay for their trip. Telok Ayer Street was next to the docks in the 1800s and one of the first streets immigrants saw when they arrived. Travellers grateful to have arrived in one piece built temples here, so Chinese temples stand alongside Indian places of worship.

WHEN RAFFLES RETURNED TO SINGAPORE IN 1822, HE SAW SUCH A MIX OF NATIONALITIES — FROM INDIAN, ARMENIAN AND EUROPEAN TO MALAYSIAN — THAT HE DECIDED EACH NEEDED A SPECIFIC PART OF THE CITY TO BUILD THEIR OWN COMMUNITY. THOSE DISTRICTS ARE MUCH THE SAME TODAY.

ECONOMICAL WITH THE TOOTH

BUDDHA TOOTH TEMPLE

An upper canine tooth of the Buddha was allegedly discovered in 1980 and brought to Singapore. Since 2007, it has been on show in a temple that's not just enormous, it's also dazzling! Pilgrims climb to the fourth floor, passing wall upon wall of elaborate works of art telling the Buddha's story, to the shrine that holds his tooth. The shrine is 3m (10ft) wide, surrounded by golden floor tiles and studded with gems. Other temples claim to have the tooth relic and some experts think it belonged to an animal, so it's hard to know what the 'tooth' is!

THERE ARE OTHER RELICS HERE, INCLUDING THE CREMATED REMAINS OF BITS OF BUDDHA'S NOSE, BRAIN AND LIVER. FOR FOLLOWERS OF THE BUDDHA, SEEING HIS RELICS IS SAID TO BE JUST AS GOOD AS SEEING THE GREAT MAN HIMSELF.

EELING HOT, HOT, HOT

RI MARIAMMAN TEMPLE

s is Singapore's oldest Hindu temple and its biggest. riamman is the goddess of fire-walking and, as part of retelling of an old Indian story, worshippers fire-walk e. A pit burns at the back of the temple, and male walkers roach it by lying on the ground and rolling sideways! They n walk barefoot across a bed of hot charcoal. It's said se who live a virtuous life should feel no pain, but most ve across the 3m (10ft) red-hot fire pit very quickly indeed, ore plunging their feet into a trench of cooling cow's milk.

SRI MARIAMMAN TEMPLE

CHINATOWN

WHO'S FOR THE SHOPHOUSE?

CHINATOWN HERITAGE CENTRE

The rows of shophouses that started springing up from the 1840s onwards were small and cramped, with just 6 sq. m (64 sq. ft) of living space for a single family, or sometimes even two! Many shophouses were knocked down in the rush to develop Singapore, but not all of them were destroyed. The Chinese Heritage Centre occupies three shophouses, and the exhibitions inside show what life was really like for people in Chinatown's rollercoaster past.

PEDAL POWER

ALL OVER CHINATOWN

When rickshaws were banned in 1947, rickshaw pullers took to pedalling trishaws instead. A trishaw is a bicycle with a third wheel that supports a small seat just big enough for two people. The first trishaws arrived in Singapore over 100 years ago, and trishaw 'uncles' operated around Chinatown, ferrying children to school, mums to market and even taking couples out on dates. There weren't many trishaws left by the end of the 1970s, but today the uncles and their bikes are back, because trishaws are perfect for sightseeing and they're eco-friendly, too.

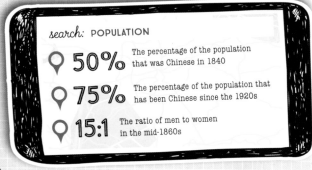

search: POPULATION

50% The percentage of the population that was Chinese in 1840

75% The percentage of the population that has been Chinese since the 1920s

15:1 The ratio of men to women in the mid-1860s

INSULTING THE SULTAN

KAMPONG GLAM

After Raffles landed in 1819, he invited a Malayan sultan, Hussein Shah, to rule the area. Shah moved to what is now Singapore with his followers and settled in the area known as Kampong Glam, but things did not run smoothly and everyone fell out. The sultan upset the British by constantly asking for more money, then the British upset the sultan by building a road right through the middle of his compound!

KAMPONG GLAM WAS DESIGNATED A MUSLIM AREA, ATTRACTING TRADERS FROM JAVA, SUMATRA AND YEMEN. TODAY IT'S A POPULAR PART OF TOWN, AND, WITH SHOPS SELLING PERSIAN CARPETS, TEXTILES AND LEATHER GOODS, IT STILL HAS A MIDDLE EASTERN FEEL.

KAMPONG GLAM

LISTEN TO THE PARROT

LITTLE INDIA

Many Indian soldiers, known as *sepoys*, and convicts were sent to Singapore as construction workers. Lots of these men stayed on, found work or started businesses, and raised families. Indians moved to this area to set up brick kilns and herd cattle, but it only got the name Little India in the 1970s. Today, its streets are busy, noisy and colourful. Much like the streets of India, the smell of incense and spices hangs in the air here. Indian shops and curry houses line the streets and in the old days you could even find fortune-telling parrots!

OLDEN ONIONS

ULTAN MOSQUE

aching up above the shophouses of Kampong Glam, Sultan Mosque's onion-shaped domes gleam in the sun. mosque was first built here for Sultan Hussein Shah in 24, but when it fell into disrepair 100 years later, this w one was commissioned. Underneath those golden nes, there's a layer of glass bottles. The sultan didn't t want the rich to have the glory of contributing wards the building of the mosque; the bottles were the ntribution of the poor.

SULTAN MOSQUE

THE FORTUNE TELLER SAT AT A TABLE, WITH A DECK OF CARDS AND A PARROT. THE CUSTOMER SAT DOWN AND THE PARROT, SENSING THE CUSTOMER'S LUCK, PICKED AN APPROPRIATE CARD. THE PARROT HOPPED BACK INTO ITS CAGE, AND THE FORTUNE TELLER USED THE CARD TO TELL THE CUSTOMER'S FORTUNE!

SHELTER FROM THE STORM

Lying just above the equator, Singapore's temperature is warm all year round and rarely dips below 24°C (75°F). The heat can be unbearable, but one thing locals are prepared for at all times is rain. While a downpour may be refreshing, it's good to be able to scurry indoors, too!

MARINA BARRAGE

WATER STORY

NEWATER VISITOR CENTRE

With so much water falling from the sky, you'd think there should be plenty to drink. But without enough land to store water, Singapore has been importing it from Malaysia since the 1960s. Plans are afoot for the city to become self-sufficient with the help of NEWater plants. Waste water is pumped to the plant via an underground sewage tunnel that's 48km (30 miles) long and converted into super-pure drinking water before it flows back into the homes and businesses it came from.

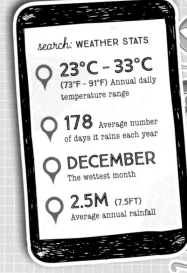

search: WEATHER STATS

📍 **23°C – 33°C** (73°F – 91°F) Annual daily temperature range

📍 **178** Average number of days it rains each year

📍 **DECEMBER** The wettest month

📍 **2.5M** (7.5FT) Average annual rainfall

GOING WITH THE FLOW

MARINA BARRAGE

Floods have been a problem in Singapore for decades, and with climate change things are getting worse. There's a danger that parts of this low-lying island could end up permanently under water! But Marina Barrage has been built to help, by directing floodwater from the city into the sea. In fact, the barrage building is so eco-friendly that it's even got a recycled plastic roof covered in soil and grass. The roof helps to heat the building below, while up on top, kids are free to fly their kites!

START

NEWATER VISITOR CENTRE

FIFTEEN FAMOUS MINUTES

FORT CANNING

This bunker, aka the Battlebox, was constructed at the start of the Second World War. It was top secret, bomb-proof and fully stocked with provisions. When the Japanese invaded Singapore in February 1942, the ruling British top brass moved here and, seven days later, it was here that they made the decision to surrender. The meeting to seal Singapore's fate lasted just 15 minutes, but it marked the beginning of the end for the centuries-old British Empire.

TOY STORY

MINT MUSEUM

With five floors to play on, each one bursting with toys from the past, this is a great place to find shelter from the storm. Visitors can cuddle up with teddies and dolls on level three, meet some crazy comic characters on level four, and travel right out of this world with the space collection on level five.

50,000
NUMBER OF TOYS IN THE COLLECTION

ANOTHER HANDY THING TO DO IN A DOWNPOUR IS HOP ON THE MRT AND ZIP ACROSS TOWN. MRT STANDS FOR MASS RAPID TRANSIT. IT IS SINGAPORE'S UNDERGROUND RAIL NETWORK. FAST AND EFFICIENT, IT HAS 119 STATIONS AND IT TRANSPORTS OVER THREE MILLION PEOPLE A DAY!

MINT MUSEUM

FORT CANNING

FRIGHTENING LIGHTNING

MERLION STATUE

When thunder rolls, lightning often strikes too, and locals seek out special shelters in parks and other outdoor areas. In fact, thunderstorms happen on average 168 days each year. It's no wonder Singapore calls itself the lightning capital of the world! No part of the island is exempt. One Saturday afternoon in 2009, there was a loud explosion as the city's famous Merlion statue was hit. The creature was left with a hole the size of a football and stopped spouting water for three long weeks!

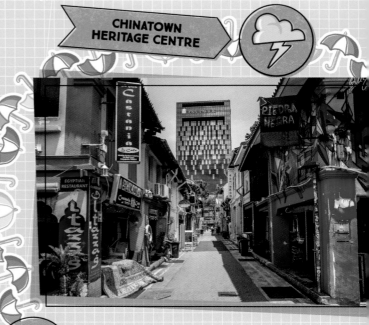

CHINATOWN HERITAGE CENTRE

MERLION STATUE

"Ouch!"

2–6PM
MOST LIKELY TIME OF DAY FOR A THUNDERSTORM

30 MINS
AVERAGE LENGTH OF A THUNDERSTORM

I SPY

CHINATOWN HERITAGE CENTRE

Singapore's shophouses were first built in the 19th century, with shops downstairs and accommodation upstairs. By law they had to have at least 1.5m (5ft) of covered space outside the ground-floor shop. These outdoor corridors are known as 'five-foot ways' and were intended as a shelter from the sun and the rain but they had another useful feature. Family rooms upstairs extended over the walkway. By removing a floor tile residents could spy on people down below and ignore unwanted customers.

SINGAPORE RAIN WILL NEVER STOP SHOPPERS. NOT WHEN AIR-CONDITIONED UNDERGROUND TUNNELS CONNECT HUNDREDS OF SHOPS ALONG ORCHARD ROAD. THERE'S EVEN AN UNDERGROUND SHOPPING MALL. SOME LOCALS CAN GO TO WORK, EAT AND SHOP WITHOUT NEEDING TO COME UP FOR AIR

TROPICAL WINTER

SNOW CITY

If any Singapore locals long for snow, there is one place they can find it all year round. In Snow City, 150 tonnes (165 sh tons) of snow covers the ground and it's 40cm (16in) deep all over. Snow City actually makes its own snow using liquid nitrogen, water and a specially designed high-pressure snow gun. Workers need to make 10 to 15 tonnes (11 to 16.5 sh tons) of snow a week to keep the level just right.

INDOOR STORM

MARITIME EXPERIENTIAL MUSEUM

One indoor attraction that might make visitors wish they'd stayed outside is the Typhoon Theatre. This experience invites up to 150 visitors on board a ship. With the help of a colossal curved screen, special moving projectors and a floor that drops from under their feet, visitors get a pretty good idea of what it's really like to be shipwrecked. It's quite scary, but luckily, the experience is only four and a half minutes long!

MARITIME
EXPERIENTIAL MUSEUM

VISITORS CLIMB THE HEIGHT OF A THREE-STOREY BUILDING TO SLIDE DOWN A SNOW SLOPE THAT'S 60M (197FT) LONG.

41

...AND RELAX

Sometimes there's just too much action going on in Singapore, so it's lucky there's no shortage of quiet corners to escape the crowds. In fact, there are loads of interesting and unusual ways to relax here, and this trail highlights just a few of them.

START

AYUR CENTRE

A LOAD OF OLD COBBLES
KATONG PARK

After a hard day's shopping, a massage could be the perfect way to soothe the feet. Reflexologists say nerve endings in the foot correspond to different parts of the body, so a foot massage has benefits all over. But walking on cobblestones could be just as good! Katong Park's reflexology walk looks beautiful and it's practical too. Stones of various shapes and sizes are set into the concrete path; all visitors have to do is kick off their shoes and walk over them slowly (and painfully!

KATONG PARK

OIL WELLNESS
AYUR CENTRE

Third-eye therapy is relaxation Indian style. The patient lies on a bed with their head back, while a warm stream of oil flows over their third eye (the area just above the gap between the eyebrows). This is said to be the part of the body where consciousness comes from, so the treatment is intended to improve blood circulation to the brain and help all kinds of conditions, from insomnia to thinking too much! There must be something in it, because this Ayurvedic treatment has been around for 5,000 years!

A CALMING CUPPA
TEA CHAPTER, CHINATOWN

There's nothing more relaxing than a nice cup of tea. Tea Chapter is Singapore's largest tea house, and a cup of tea here is treated like a fine wine, its flavour varying according to the variety: black, green, white, yellow, oolong or floral. Then there's the various roasting or fermentation processes and the type of pot and cup it's served in. Even a tea-maker's mood is important – tea brewed by someone who's stressed won't taste nearly so good!

Customers are advised to drink their tea in three sips:

> **a small sip first, to check the heat**
> **a second larger sip to get the flavour**
> **a third big sip to finish it off fast!**

CHINATOWN

PLENTY OF VIPS HAVE VISITED TEA CHAPTER, BUT ONE OF THE FIRST WAS QUEEN ELIZABETH II, WHO CAME SOON AFTER THE SHOP OPENED. CUSTOMERS CAN STILL SAMPLE THE OOLONG THE QUEEN SIPPED ALL THOSE YEARS AGO.

HERAPY? IT'S FISHY!

ENKO WELLNESS, CHINATOWN POINT

stomers dip their feet, arms, legs or whole body (if they're ve) into a tank of water and the fish tuck in! Hundreds hem nibble away the dead skin and allow the layers below to glow! nay tickle a little, but these are doctor fish and they don't bite – y haven't got any teeth! The fish come from Turkey, along with therapy, which has been helping to heal skin conditions there for over 100 years. The idea isn't new here either – Kenko Wellness has offered fishy treatments for over 20 years.

CHESSMATES
CHINATOWN COMPLEX

Chinese chess, or *xiangqi*, is traditionally played by Singapore's older generation. At the Chinatown Complex, there are many fixed tables and chairs where two friends can do battle. The board looks like a simple grid and it's usually etched into the tabletop. Some of the pieces are different from Western-style chess pieces – like the chariot, cannon and elephant – and they move in different ways, too, providing lots more possibilities. The Chinese say their chess is way harder than the Western version!

LEARNING *XIANGQI* IS GOOD FOR THE BRAIN, AND SCHOOL CHILDREN ARE ENCOURAGED TO GIVE IT A GO. IT CAN HELP WITH MEMORY AND CONCENTRATION, AS WELL AS IMPROVING YOUR INTELLIGENCE – APPARENTLY!

CHINATOWN COMPLEX

KADAMPA MEDITATION CENTRE

ALL IN THE MIND
KADAMPA MEDITATION CENTRE

In a city as fast moving as Singapore, it's easy to go into information overload. The perfect antidote to that is a class at the meditation centre. Students sit in a quiet room, cross-legged on the floor, backs straight, eyes half closed, breathing through the nose and – here comes the difficult bit – try to turn off the chatter in their heads. It may take a few attempts, but it's got to be worth the effort because, according to Buddha, this is the way to find true happiness.

SINGAPORE SINGS
TANG MUSIC BOX

[Ev]en tone-deaf wallflowers can find themselves [gr]abbing the mic and belting out a familiar [tun]e in front of friends and family when [the]re'a a karaoke machine nearby. Being able [to s]ing isn't what karaoke is about; it's more [to d]o with having fun. There's a wide range of [kar]aoke bars in Singapore, from ones that look [lik]e your granny's lounge to Tang Music Box, [wit]h rooms big enough for parties of 40 people, [str]obe lighting, stylish décor and [larg]e screens. No matter where you [dec]ide to go, the biggest factor is [alw]ays the range of songs.

search: SILENCE

⦿ RETREAT

If normal meditation doesn't go far enough, people who want true peace and quiet can head to St. John's Island. While taking part in a ten-day silent retreat, everyone has to hand over their mobile phones or any other way of communicating with the outside world!

25 🎤
ROOMS

⏰ CLOSES 3–6 AM

100,000+
SONGS
[I]N VARIOUS LANGUAGES [I]NCLUDING ENGLISH, [M]ANDARIN, CANTONESE, [K]OREAN AND JAPANESE

ORTO

GONE FISHIN'
ORTO

Singaporeans are hooked on prawn fishing. Would-be prawn-catchers start by hiring a rod and net and choosing their bait — chicken heart or worms, perhaps? Then they sit beside a prawning pond, drop in the hook and line, and wait. If the float dips below the surface for five seconds, they have a catch! Patience is rewarded at the grill nearby, with prawns on sticks for supper, breakfast or even a midnight feast, because prawn fishing goes on at Orto 24 hours a day!

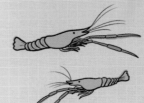

TANG MUSIC BOX

RAINBOW CITY

With all that sunshine and rain, Singapore gets its fair share of rainbows. Down on the ground, there's colour all around the city, from tropical fruit such as purple mangosteens on market stalls, to red stripes on a temple, and there's never a shortage of greenery...

VERTICAL VEGETABLES

SKY GREENS

Everything's green in this sky-high greenhouse. With farmland in short supply and skyscrapers solving the housing problem, growing vegetables in the sky is a no-brainer. The veggies grow in rows of troughs supported on triangular metal frames up to 9m (30ft) tall. Recycled rainwater powers the towers – before it's used to water the plants – and the towers rotate to give each plant two hours of sunlight and three glugs of water per day. The sky farm is green in another way too: the towers have no emissions because each one only uses the same energy as a 40-watt lightbulb.

DREAM SCHOOL

NANYANG PRIMARY SCHOOL

Plain white classrooms in this school help children concentrate in lessons. But rushing out of the classroom door is like walking into a dream. The kids are met with a kaleidoscope of colour! The school buildings create a kind of valley, with bridges standing on striking yellow columns, green garden spaces in the courtyard below and bright horizontal rainbow stripes running all along the walls! If the kids designed the school themselves, it would probably look just like this!

LIGHTS FANTASTIC

LITTLE INDIA

This part of Singapore is a bright place at the best of times, but at Diwali, it's brighter and shinier than ever. During the Hindu festival of lights, buildings, homes and streets are illuminated in every colour. At home, doorsteps are swept and vibrant *rangoli* patterns are made to welcome in Lakshmi, the goddess of wealth. *Rangoli* are traditionally made from rice, flour, coloured powders and flowers, but in 2016, artist Vijaya Mohan made a super-sized *rangoli* at Gardens by the Bay using marbles and other items.

10 X 12M (33 X 39 FT) SIZE OF THE RANGOLI

15,000
Number of marbles in Vijaya Mohan's rangoli. She also used glitter and coloured paper.

MELLOW YELLOW

JOO CHIAT, KATONG

Colourful shophouses brighten up many districts of the city, but these Peranakan properties are some of the prettiest. They're decorated in delicate pastel shades, with Peranakan motifs of flowers and mythical creatures. The shophouses didn't always look so lively. When they were first built they were plastered off-white. The first coloured shophouses were deep blue and yellowy brown, because indigo and ochre were the only colours available. Today, any colour goes, from deep red, to purple, to gold!

TOWER OF COLOUR

SRI VEERAMAKALIAMMAN TEMPLE

Sri Veeramakaliamman is one of the oldest temples in Singapore and by far the most colourful. The huge entrance gate on the front of the red-and-white-striped temple building is crammed with painted statues and balanced on four bright blue pillars.

DEDICATED GODDESS

The temple is built to the goddess Sri Veeramakaliamman, or Kali for short. One of the temple statues shows her blue body naked, with a string of skulls round her neck and human heads and hands dangling from her belt! She is sometimes shown with many hands to help her destroy evil, but she's actually not as scary as she looks. Kali is also said to be a loving mother, protecting her worshippers as if they were children, so she was the perfect goddess for immigrants arriving in a foreign land.

KALI OFTEN HAS HER TONGUE STICKING OUT! ALTHOUGH IT MAKES HER LOOK FIERCE, IT'S OFTEN INTERPRETED AS A SIGN OF HER

NEW BEGINNINGS

The temple started out with a shrine to a small clay statue of Sri Veeramakaliamman, which was eventually replaced by a finer statue shipped over from India. Gradually, more statues arrived, and as rooms were built to house them, so the temple expanded. Workers began rebuilding the temple in 1983, adding the brilliant new gateway, eight large domes and several smaller ones. But as they cleared the ground for the shiny new temple, they came across some old clay statues from the very first shrine that had stood there over 150 years earlier.

SRI VEERAMAKALIAMMAN TEMPLE

640
NUMBER OF STATUES OF HINDU GODS IN AND AROUND THE TEMPLE

3 YEARS
THE TIME IT TOOK TO BUILD THE POWER

SHE'S DEPICTED IN DIFFERENT COLOURS AND WITH DIFFERENT NUMBERS OF HANDS AND EYES.

FLOWER POWER

HINDU VISITORS HANG FLOWER GARLANDS AROUND THE STATUES IN THE TEMPLE AS A WAY OF HONOURING THEIR GODS. DIFFERENT GODS HAVE DIFFERENT GARLANDS. KALI IS OFFERED ONES MADE FROM NEEM LEAVES, WHICH HAVE SPECIAL MEDICINAL PROPERTIES, WHILE GANESHA, HER SON, GETS NOT-SO-SPECIAL-LOOKING GRASS GARLANDS!

SMASHING COCONUTS

Coconuts are often used as offerings in Hindu temples. On their way in to the Sri Veeramakaliamman Temple in Singapore, worshippers can stop at a special box to smash one! Breaking the coconut symbolises the smashing of the ego — it's a way of people showing that they are humble.

SWEET SUCCESS

RESIDENCE OF TAN TENG NIAH

With all kinds of colours decorating the outside of this building, it seems appropriate that its original owner ran sweet-making factories. It's probable that when Tan first built the villa in 1900, the roof was plain green and the walls just white. Tan was Chinese, but he built this house in Little India, so it's more recently been given a makeover, Indian style, and has become a popular photo opportunity with tourists.

RESIDENCE OF TAN TENG NIAH

STAYING FRESH

BUFFALO ROAD

Singapore street names often tell a story and Buffalo Road is no exception. Indian cattle herders once brought their cows and goats door to door along this road to provide milk for its residents – and it doesn't come much fresher than that! Today, fresh produce still fills the street, but the cattle are long gone and it's a riot of colour here instead. Fruit and vegetable stalls sell everything from deep-purple mangosteens (tropical fruit) to bright-green okra (podded vegetable) and spicy red chillies, while fragrant flower stalls are hung with garlands of roses, jasmine and marigolds.

GARLANDS AREN'T JUST USED FOR GODS AND GODDESSES IN THE TEMPLES. WOMEN WEAR THEM IN THEIR HAIR. A BRIDE AND GROOM GIVE GARLANDS TO EACH OTHER AT THEIR WEDDING, AND WHEN VERY IMPORTANT PEOPLE ARRIVE SOMEWHERE, THEY ARE OFTEN PRESENTED WITH A BRIGHT-ORANGE OR YELLOW GARLAND THAT'S ALMOST AS TALL AS THEY ARE.

HIDDEN HOTEL
PARKROYAL ON PICKERING

Plenty of high-rises have sky gardens, but no other sky gardens are quite like these! The Parkroyal on Pickering hotel drips with greenery. Its shape means all the rooms either look out at a park or at plants growing on balconies around the building. The plants keep the building cool, and all of the overhanging vegetation conveniently hides an ugly car park. It also allows hotel guests total privacy – except when gardeners pop up to tend the plants.

search: PARK ROYAL

0 Amount of energy used to power the gardens: solar lights turn on automatically and all rainwater is collected and recycled

680 The number of households that could be powered by the hotel's yearly energy savings

32+ Number of swimming pools that could be filled with the rainwater the hotel conserves each year

ROBERTSON QUAY

PARKROYAL ON PICKERING

OAT OF MANY COLOURS
KAFF BRIDGE, ROBERTSON QUAY

kaff Bridge is designed to look like a traditional *tongkang* rgo boat. Artist Pacita Abad loved its shape but wasn't keen the colour: battleship grey. She persuaded the authorities that e should give it a many-coloured coat of paint. And in 2004, eam of people turned the bridge blue, green, yellow, pink and , before the tricky business began of adding circle and spiral tterns. Abad was known for her big, bold paintings, but this s the biggest, boldest painting of her life.

SADLY, ABAD DIED IN 2004, NOT LONG AFTER THE BRIDGE WAS PAINTED, BUT SHE'S REMEMBERED IN SINGAPORE AS THE 'BRIDGE LADY'. ONE OF HER AL WISHES WAS THAT EVERYONE WHO WALKED ACROSS THE BRIDGE SHOULD SMILE AND ENJOY HER ART.

WATER WAY TO GO

In the 19th century, the Dutch dominated Southeast Asian waters. The British wanted to control the Strait of Malacca to give their ships an easier route to the South China Sea. Raffles spotted the perfect place for a harbour at Singapore. Today, the sea is still Singapore's greatest asset – not just for trade but for fun too!

1 MILLION
NUMBER OF PEOPL[E]
VISITING SINGAPOR[E]
BY CRUISE SHI[P]
EACH YEAR

385
CRUISE SHIPS THA[T]
DOCK EACH YEAR

START

SENTOSA

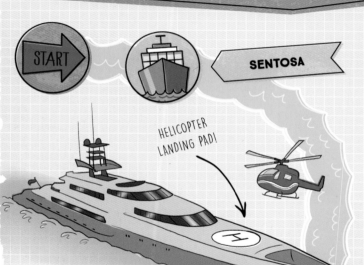

HELICOPTER LANDING PAD!

JUST CRUISIN'

CRUISE CENTRE SINGAPORE, MARINA BAY

Singapore's newest cruise centre is really close to the city's hotspots and built to welcome some of the largest cruise ships in the world, such as the *AIDAperla*, pictured below. The cruise centre is the size of three football fields, with a roof that looks like breaking waves! Its largest visitor, *Ovation of the Seas*, is a whopping 348m (1,142ft) long and, with over 2,000 cabins, it can accommodate up to 4,905 guests.

SHIP SHAPE

COVE AVENUE, SENTOSA

The Singapore Yacht Show is a must-see for the city's many millionaires, but anyone can sneak a peek at some of the world's newest superyachts. In 2017, the largest on display was the *Silver Fast*, a boat that looks like it should feature in a James Bond movie. On board there's a gym, sauna, hot tub, cinema and space to accommodate up to 18 guests! And for anyone needing a superfast getaway, the *Silver Fast* even has a helipad!

MARINA BAY

A LIFE ON THE OCEAN WAVE

SINGAPORE RIVER

In the early 1800s, around 1,000 Orang Laut people lived on the waters around Singapore in houseboats called *sampans*. The Orang Laut were here before everybody else. Babies were born, couples were married, and people even died in their boats. Those living around the river mouth started making a living selling food to merchant ships. But as river traffic grew busier, the *sampans* were pushed out, and by 1840 many of the Orang Laut had been forced to move on.

UTSIDE THE BOX

NGAPORE MARITIME GALLERY, ARINA SOUTH PIER

gapore opened a new port for container ships in 1972. ween 2005 and 2010, this was the busiest port in the rld, and today it's still number two (after Shanghai in na). A ship arrives or leaves here every two to three nutes. Singapore doesn't have many goods of its own rade, but ships stop here to change cargo or refuel. e Maritime Gallery tells visitors all about it — they even walk through a shipping container and have o at steering a ship (but not a real one)!

SOME OF THE ORANG LAUT WERE PIRATES, AND WHEN WILLIAM FARQUHAR, SINGAPORE'S FIRST BRITISH RESIDENT, DISCOVERED HUMAN SKULLS ON THE ISLAND, HE ASKED THE ORANG LAUT HOW THEY HAD GOT THERE. THEY ALLEGEDLY SAID THE HEADS WERE FROM MEN WHO HAD BEEN ROBBED AT SEA AND BROUGHT ON LAND TO BE KILLED!

,000
MBER OF SHIPS
THE PORT AT
NY ONE TIME

130,000
NUMBER OF SHIPS
THAT CALL AT THE
PORT EACH YEAR

BOATFACE

MERLION PARK

For around 150 years, *tongkangs* (also known as bumboats) dominated the waters of the Singapore River. These light boats ferried goods from merchant ships that docked in the outer harbour to and from the city's warehouses. When bridges were built along the river, some of the boats were too tall to pass underneath, and eventually they were removed from this part of the river altogether. But today, the *tongkangs* are back, working as water taxis, or used for sightseeing cruises. It's easy to spot one – eyes painted on the front are always looking out for trouble.

FLOWIN' SLOW

SINGAPORE RIVER

The mouth of the Singapore River formed the city's first harbour. Over the years, the combination of river traffic, industries, and hawker stalls on the riverbank led to huge problems with pollution. The water was full of rubbish, sewage and even abandoned boats. In fact, there was so much rubbish that the river turned black and ships found it difficult to navigate along it. In 1977, Prime Minister Lee Kuan Yew decided the stinking waters needed a clean up. Ten years later, fish and prawns were happily splashing about in the river once again.

SINGAPORE RIVER

UNKEN TREASURE

IAN CIVILISATIONS MUSEUM

k in the 9th century, tragedy struck a Middle Eastern ship south of Singapore
nd and it lay under water until fishermen discovered it in 1998. The ship's
go was so well packed that much of it survived intact, including silver boxes,
len bowls, bronze mirrors and more than 50,000 mass-produced pottery bowls
display in this museum)! People used to believe that trade between the Middle
t and Asia was only overland, but this wreck proves that a watery trade route
sted over 1,000 years ago – well before the Europeans found their way here!

CLARKE QUAY

QUAYS TO THE CITY

CLARKE QUAY

In the 1900s, Boat Quay, Clarke
Quay and Robertson Quay were
jammed with *tongkangs* carrying
a wealth of cargoes. Workers
ran along wobbly gangplanks,
hoisting sacks onto their shoulders
and hurrying with their loads
to the warehouses, or *godowns*.
Today, new uses have been found
for many *godowns* and Clarke
Quay is a top destination with
shops and restaurants packed
into the old warehouses.

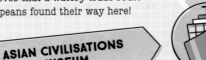

ASIAN CIVILISATIONS
MUSEUM

90 NUMBER OF RIVERS
IN SINGAPORE

3.2KM LENGTH OF
(2 MILES) SINGAPORE RIVER

search: WASTE WATER

SINGAPORE INTERNATIONAL WATER WEEK

Singaporeans use an incredible
amount of water every single
day – enough to fill the
equivalent of 782 Olympic-sized
swimming pools! During
Singapore International Water
Week, people from around
the globe come together to
discuss how to look after water
so there's enough for everyone.

CHOOSE YOUR ISLAND

Because it isn't controlled by any other country, Singapore is known as an 'island state'. It's also nicknamed the Little Red Dot, because on some maps, the island is so small that it's covered up by the dot that marks its place in the world. In fact, Singapore isn't just one 'dot', it's surrounded by 62 other islands, or *pulau*, as they're called in Malay. Each island has its own story to tell.

PULAU SATUMU

HIGH LIGHTS

PULAU SATUMU

This island is so small that its nam *Satumu* translates as 'one tree'. At first engineers didn't think it could support the weight of a 29m (95ft) lighthouse. It was in the perfect posi to protect ships entering the Western Singapore Straits, however, so up the structure went, and it's been working since 1855. Seven men were once nee to man the lighthouse, instead of the t it takes today, and the kerosene lamps old have been replaced with halogen la powered by solar energy.

COME TOGETHER

JURONG ISLAND

Land reclamation has been happening in Singapore ever since Raffles arrived, but new land hasn't just been created on Singapore Island itself. In the 1960s and 70s, work began to reclaim swampland in the Jurong area for industry and shipping. Nearby islands were enlarged and finally, in the 1990s, seven islands were joined together to create one big one: Jurong Island, which was officially opened in 2000.

Jurong Island   Pulau Ubin

Pulau Semakau   Sentosa

Kusu Island

Lazarus Island

St. John's Island

Pulau Satumu

37KM
(20 NAUTICAL MILES)

DISTANCE THE LIGHTHOUSE BEAM TRAVELS

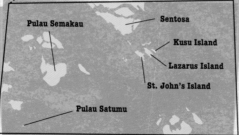

JURONG ISLAND

RUBBISH TRIP

PULAU SEMAKAU

A trip to Singapore's latest landfill island may not sound exciting, but visitors are astonished by how beautiful the site is! There's no smell and no sign of any rubbish, because the whole place has been carefully developed with ecology in mind. A 7km (4 mile) wall built out into the sea encloses cells that are filled with waste one by one, then covered with topsoil so that plants and birds will settle on top. Today, sea anemones, barracuda and great-billed herons can be found here, and in 2014 a very rare giant sponge was discovered right in the landfill lagoon!

BECAUSE OF ITS SHAPE, THE GIANT SPONGE IS KNOWN AS NEPTUNE'S CUP. FIRST DISCOVERED IN 1822, SOME OF THESE SPONGES WERE SO BIG THEY WERE ACTUALLY USED AS BATHTUBS FOR CHILDREN. SADLY, BY THE 1870s THERE WERE HARDLY ANY LEFT AROUND SINGAPORE. THE 2014 DISCOVERY WAS ONLY THE SECOND NEPTUNE'S CUP FOUND ALIVE SINCE 1908!

COOL FOR CATS

ST. JOHN'S ISLAND

When the port of Singapore first opened for business, flags flown on this island signalled for passing ships to drop anchor so a boat could row out and tell them all about the place. Then, after 357 people died of cholera in Singapore in 1873, a quarantine hospital was built on this island. Ships reported here before docking in Singapore, and any sick passengers were left behind for treatment. There's been a prison and a prisoner-of-war camp here, but hardly any humans live here now. Instead, it's home to around 100 friendly cats!

ST. JOHN'S ISLAND

57

TURTLY SACRED

KUSU ISLAND

Kusu means turtle in the local Hokkien dialect and there's an interesting legend behind the name. Two sailors, one Chinese, one Malay, were shipwrecked and struggling for their lives, when a giant turtle saved them – by turning itself into an island! Kusu has been a place of worship ever since, and every year, between September and November, a month-long religious festival attracts around 100,000 people to this otherwise quiet island! Visitors have to jump on a boat at the end of the day, though – nobody is allowed to stay overnight on Kusu.

search: DESERT ISLANDS

📍 KEEP OFF!

Three islands locals definitely aren't allowed to visit are Senang, Pawai and Sudong. They lie in shark-infested waters for a start, and there's a search here every morning to check for trespassers. Once the coast is clear, the action begins as aircraft zoom overhead dropping bombs down below. But this isn't the start of World War III, these islands are used as target practice for the Singapore Air Force fighter planes!

KUSU ISLAND

LAZARUS ISLAND

DESERTED ISLAND

LAZARUS ISLAND

No ferries stop off at Lazarus Island, so visitors who don't have their own private yacht usually wander across the bridge from St. John's Island in the company of a few stray cats. There are no shops or cafés here either, and there's nowhere to stay, but unlike many busier spots on the Singapore coastline, there is clear water and a beautiful, quiet, unspoilt beach.

BACK IN TIME

PULAU UBIN

Arriving by *tongkang* at Pulau Ubin is a bit like travelling back in time. Some people say that this island is exactly how parts of Singapore used to be. There are no tarmacked roads, no concrete buildings and definitely no skyscrapers. Around 100 people still live here in tin-roofed wooden houses on stilts. Wild boar roam the forests, durian fruit grow on trees and there are insects that can bite right through a layer or two of clothing!

TION-PACKED

TOSA ISLAND

ppers arrive on Sentosa by car, monorail,
ar, luxury yacht, or by simply walking
the bridge! But forget peace and quiet,
and is action-packed! The Tiger Sky
takes visitors up 50 storeys in a revolving
o reveal amazing views of Singapore and
islands. At the Universal Studios theme
here are roller-coaster rides based on films
s *Revenge of the Mummy*, *Transformers*
rek. And the SEA Aquarium is one of
gest in the world! Some people come
enjoy the beach.

PULAU UBIN

24 RIDES AND ATTRACTIONS

2.5M HEIGHT OF WORLD'S TALLEST DUELLING
39FT) ROLLERCOASTER

THE AQUARIUM ON SENTOSA HAS 49 HABITATS TO EXPLORE. THERE'S A SHIPWRECK TEEMING WITH MARINE LIFE FROM THE JAVA SEA AND YOU CAN SEE SCALLOPED HAMMERHEAD SHARKS IN THE SHARK SEAS HABITAT. THE OPEN OCEAN HABITAT HAS ONE OF THE LARGEST VIEWING PANELS IN THE WORLD — IT'S 36M (118FT) WIDE AND 8.3M (27FT) HIGH! LEOPARD SHARKS, SAW FISH AND SQUADRONS OF MANTA RAY SWIM SILENTLY PAST BEHIND THE GLASS.

THE DARK SIDE

With weddings for the dead, a theme park attraction based on hell and mobile phones in the afterlife, this trail is not for the faint-hearted!

PULAU HANTU

HELL ON EARTH

HAW PAR VILLA

Aw Boon Haw built this villa for his younger brother, Boon Par, in the 1930s and its gardens became a theme park for Chinese mythology. But rumours say the statues here are really dead bodies covered in wax! The Ten Courts of Hell exhibit is particularly gruesome, with sculptures showing graphic scenes of the terrible punishments awaiting sinners after death! It's said that once the sun sets the statues come to life. Night guards claim they've heard screams coming from the exhibit, which is why they leave offerings such as food by certain statues, hoping for protection.

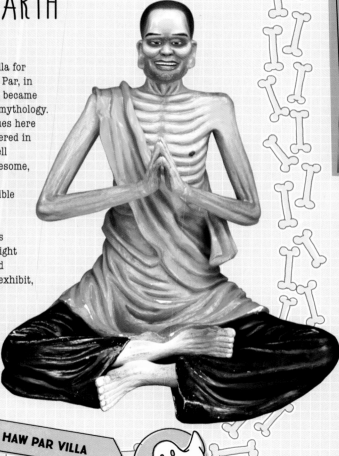

GHOST ISLANDS

PULAU HANTU

Today, visitors dive and snorkel in the peaceful waters around the island of Pulau Hantu, but according to legend, it has a vi and bloody past! Two mighty warriors, (bigger than the other, were once caught in a battle to rule the seas. Many of the soldiers died and the sea turned red with blood. Furious sea genies sent a whirlpool drown the warriors, but they kept fighting until they stabbed each other and died. The sea genies turned them into two connected islands – one large, one small. At low tide you can wade from one to the other.

START

HAW PAR VILLA

CORPSE BRIDE
SENG WONG BEO TEMPLE

In the Chinese Tao religion, it's believed that if an unmarried person comes back to haunt their family, it's probably because they're searching for a husband or wife! At Seng Wong Beo Temple, anxious relatives can exchange photos in a bid to find a perfect dead partner for their lost loved ones. Once the match is made, a ceremony is conducted with a bride and groom made out of paper! After that, the spirits should calm down because they now have a higher status in the afterlife!

SAGO LANE

SENG WONG BEO TEMPLE

END OF THE ROAD
SAGO LANE

Sago Lane was once better known by the Chinese locals as Dead People Street. The shophouses nearby were crammed with residents. They didn't have room for the dying, and it was bad luck if someone died at home. So the sick came to this street to live out their final days in its death houses. The street was where the funeral would be organised too, so while sick people spent their last days upstairs, coffins and shrines were being made downstairs. Chinese funeral processions set off from Sago Lane right up until the 1960s.

search: SAGO

📍 WHAT'S IN A NAME?

Sago is a kind of starch that comes from the sago palm tree. It can be rolled into balls, made into pancakes and boiled with water or milk and sugar to make a yummy pudding. Sago Lane gets its name from the many sago factories that used to be in this area.

DEAD RICH

NAM'S SUPPLIES, CHINATOWN

Nam's Supplies sells laptops, mobile phones, Gucci handbags... there's nothing sinister about that, of course. But these items aren't for the living, they're for the dead, and they aren't real, they're made out of paper! Singaporean Chinese honour their dead relatives by taking gifts to their shrines for burning. The idea is that the dead can use these gifts in the afterlife and have a much better time. For anything invented after a loved one died, it's best to send the instructions up in smoke too!

ARCHAEOLOGISTS SAY THAT SPIRIT MONEY (ALSO KNOWN AS 'HELL MONEY') HAS BEEN OFFERED AT CHINESE SHRINES SINCE 1000 BC! OBJECTS MADE OF WOOD OR CLAY WERE OFFERED, TOO, BUT OVER TIME, PAPER VERSIONS BECAME MORE POPULAR. MOURNERS STARTED OFFERING PAPER HOUSES, CLOTHES AND EVEN SERVANTS!

DO FEED THE GHOSTS!

CHINATOWN

During the Hungry Ghost Festival, the souls of the dead are said to roam Earth, getting up to all sorts of mischief. Paper offerings are burned and food is left out on little altars to keep the ghosts happy. There's entertainment too, and the festival can be tons of f[un] but there are a few guidelines (see the box below).

GHOUL RULES:

> **STAY AWAY FROM WATER.**
Ghosts are said to cause drownings.

> **DON'T GO OUT AFTER DARK.**
Ghosts are at their most powerful then.

> **DON'T SIT IN THE FRONT ROW AT CONCERTS.**
Those seats are reserved for... guess who?

BEWARE OF THE STAIRS

NATIONAL MUSEUM

The spiral staircase that leads onto the roof of this museum isn't open to visitors any more, but even if it was they probably couldn't climb it. People say there's a mysterious force that stops anyone from getting to the top, tripping them up when they try. Some claim they've seen a priest-like figure or a long-dead museum director standing on the steps, and even the cleaners feel uneasy. That's why the museum has agreed that they only need to clean the staircase twice a week!

GHOST WRITER

NATIONAL LIBRARY

According to the National Library, Russell Lee's *True Singapore Ghost Stories* are read more than any other books in Singapore. Lee researched and published his first book back in 1989, and by 2017, there were 26 titles in the series! There's been a TV series and the books are bestsellers in Malaysia and Brunei, but there's a mystery surrounding the author. No one knows who Russell Lee really is. He only ever appears with a mask over his face and gloves on his hands. Is he some sort of ghost himself?

1.5 MILLION
NUMBER OF BOOKS
IN THE SERIES
SOLD WORLDWIDE

NATIONAL LIBRARY

BEHIND BARS

CHANGI PRISON MUSEUM

These days Changi is probably best known for its airport, but there's a prison here as well, and terrible things happened there and around this area during the Second World War.

600 NUMBER OF INMATES **THE PRISON WAS DESIGNED TO HOLD**

2,400 NUMBER OF INMATES HELD AT CHANGI PRISON DURING THE WAR

PRISON CONDITIONS

Both soldiers and civilians were imprisoned at Changi during the war. The prisoners were forced to work for meagre food rations, loading ammunition onto ships and clearing the sewers. They were beaten for not working hard enough, and living five or six to one cell meant disease spread quickly – malaria and dysentery were rife.

THE PAINTINGS ON THE WALL

One prisoner, Stanley Warren – a poster designer in peace time – was asked to decorate the chapel's walls. Like many of the men, Stanley was seriously ill at the time and too weak to work for more than 15 minutes at a stretch, and materials were almost impossible to find. Prisoners scavenged red, brown and white paint and billiard chalk, and Stanley used them to complete five amazing murals.

CHANGI PRISON

FIGHTING SPIRIT

Women and children were sent to a separate prison camp at Changi. Aged just ten, Olga Morris was made to work in the baking heat, picking vegetables she wasn't allowed to eat. Prisoners lived on rice and water and took turns to sleep on stone beds in overcrowded cells. Using thread and scraps of fabric from their dresses, Olga and her friends started making a patchwork quilt. They did it in secret, though – if the girls heard the guards coming, they'd hide their handiwork in their knickers!

BOYS WERE ALLOWED TO STAY IN THE CAMP WITH THEIR MUMS, BUT THE MOMENT THEY TURNED 12, THEY WERE PACKED OFF ALONE TO THE MEN'S PRISON.

HOSPITAL OF HORROR

TODAY, THE BUILDINGS OF OLD CHANGI HOSPITAL STAND EMPTY, AND GHOST HUNTERS CLAIM THIS IS ONE OF THE MOST HAUNTED PLACES IN THE WORLD! IT'S THOUGHT MANY MEN WERE TORTURED AND DIED HERE. A MALAYAN *PONTIANAK* IS SAID TO HAUNT THE HOSPITAL. IT'S A FEMALE GHOST WHO LURES MALE VICTIMS WITH HER BEAUTY, THEN TURNS INTO A HIDEOUS CREATURE AND ATTACKS THEM!

NOT JUST NOODLES

Singaporeans take their food very seriously indeed, and with dishes available from so many cultures, choosing what to eat can be a tricky business. From a sweet, eggy breakfast to dinner served on a leaf, here's a trail to satisfy all rumbling tums...

START · **CHINATOWN COMPLEX**

KNOW YOUR NOODLES

NOODLE MAN, CHINATOWN

Noodles come in many shapes and sizes, from delicately thin rice noodles, to wide, flat egg noodles, but customers here don't just get great noodles, they get a floor show, too! While people wait and watch, the Noodle Man makes the dough, twirling it, twisting it, spinning it like a skipping rope and slapping it on the counter. With a quick dusting of flour, he pulls the noodles into thin strands, and then they spend a few minutes in the pot before landing on a plate. Noodles don't come much fresher than that!

CHINATOWN

FINGER-LICKIN' GOOD

HONG KONG SOYA SAUCE CHICKEN AND RICE NOODLE, CHINATOWN COMPLEX

Hawker food (street food) has been sold in Singapore since the 1800s. It used to refer to food sold from a roadside cart or stall, but all stalls moved to special centres from the 1970s to improve hygiene standards. The food quality has improved so much that in 2016, the Michelin Guide awarded a star to two of Singapore's hawker stalls! And with dishes like Soya Chicken Rice selling at just S$2 (£1.11), the stalls sell the cheapest Michelin-approved meals in the world!

House of Lakes

Ah Lom Abalone

TELL IT LIKE IT IS
TELOK AYER MARKET

Also known as Lau Pa Sat, this is one of Singapore's oldest markets, though it's actually been a hawker centre since 1972. The stalls don't have fancy names, and there are hardly any chain restaurants here. Instead, the shop signs tell customers exactly what's on offer, with names such as: Indian Food, Cold Beverages and even Pig's Organ Soup!

MARKETS ARE ESPECIALLY BUSY AT LUNCHTIME, AND IT'S NOT UNUSUAL TO SHARE TABLES WITH STRANGERS. THE STALLS ARE SELF-SERVICE, SO A PACKET OF TISSUES ON A PLASTIC CHAIR IS A WAY OF SAYING 'THIS PLACE IS TAKEN'. THE PRACTICE IS CALLED *CHOPING* AND CUSTOMERS CAN *CHOPE* WITH ANYTHING THEY LIKE.

TELOK AYER MARKET

CE AND TASTY

CHINATOWN FOOD STREET, CHINATOWN

he Singapore Food Festival happens every July, and e 50 Cents Festival has to be a highlight. It's really trip down memory lane, back to the Chinatown of ears gone by, when a cup of coffee only cost 5¢ (3p). d-style dishes are all priced just 50¢ (28p), and ice balls are firm favourite. Moulded by hand from ice shavings, filled th sweet red beans and jelly, they're then drizzled with lourful syrups and a coating of evaporated milk. Mmm.

EGGY SOLDIERS

YA KUN KAYA TOAST, CHINA STREET

When Singaporeans need to get themselves going in the mornings, they'll stop off for a Singapore-style breakfast of *kaya toast*. Thick slices of bread are grilled over a charcoal flame and sandwiched together with generous slatherings of butter and kaya jam (made from eggs, sugar and coconut milk). Ya Kun's *kaya toast* comes with soft-boiled eggs. Customers crack the eggs in a bowl, and swirl them into the perfect dip for their kaya toast soldiers.

CHINA STREET

HIGH KICKING

RAFFLES HOTEL

Though British rule is long gone, Singaporeans still enjoy an English high tea, and Raffles is the classiest place to eat one. Tables in its Tiffin Room are laid with white linen cloths, and there are fine china cups, silver tea sets and three-tiered cake stands groaning with sandwiches, scones and cake. As if that's not enough, a buffet table offers Chinese dim sum, pies, sausage rolls and yet more cakes and scones. As customers hold onto their stuffed bellies, they're entertained by a harpist!

RAFFLES HOTEL

INVENTED BY INDIAN MIGRANTS, *TEH TARIK*, OR 'PULLED TEA', IS DRUNK ACROSS SINGAPORE. USING BOILING WATER WITH A TABLESPOON OF BLACK TEA LEAVES AND ONE AND A HALF TABLESPOONS OF SWEETENED CONDENSED MILK PER CUP, THE *TEH* SELLERS 'PULL' OR STRETCH THE TEA BY POURING IT FROM ONE CONTAINER INTO ANOTHER. THE LONGER THE STREAM OF TEA, THE BETTER, BECAUSE 'PULLING' THE TEA MAKES IT FABULOUSLY FROTHY!

BANANA LEAF APOLO

LEAN PLATES

ANANA LEAF APOLO

his Indian restaurant is way ahead of the game – it's been
rving curries and sambals (hot sauces) on recyclable,
degradable plates ever since it opened in 1974. The plates are
tually banana leaves, and the practice is an Indian tradition.
e leaf plates aren't just good for the environment, they're good
r human health too. They kill bacteria that can cause disease
d contain antioxidants that
p fight cancer. Best of all,
ough, there's no need to
sh up after eating!

FAB CRAB

ROLAND RESTAURANT

In the 1950s, Madam Cher and her husband, Mr Lim,
came up with a recipe for crab served in tomato sauce
with chilli. Friends and family loved it, so they started
selling it from a handcart. The handcart became a shack,
the shack became a restaurant, and the dish became
a national favourite. Other restaurants caught on to
the idea and one chef added egg to the sauce. Today
chilli crab is one of Singapore's best-loved meals, and
it's been voted one of the top 50 foods in the world!

1,100 Number of seats in Roland
Restaurant, run by Madam Cher's
son, which still serves chilli crab
made from the original recipe

search: HAWKER TALK

📍 **HAWKER** – person who travels around
selling food

📍 **HAWKER STALL** – cheap cooked-food stall
(Singapore has around 6,000 of these)

📍 **HAWKER CENTRE** – cooked-food market
(Singapore has over 100 of these)

ROLAND RESTAURANT

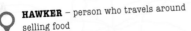

SINGAPORE STYLE

Proud of its past and looking forward to the future, Singapore is stylish in many different ways. From colourful history murals to a giant red-hot chilli pepper, the city boasts a style all of its very own.

A PROPER JOB

THIAN HOCK KENG TEMPLE

Yip Yew Chong's street art is dotted all over Singapore. So far, he has covered more than 25 walls with detailed murals showing scenes from Singapore's past. The mural on the back wall of this temple is one of the most impressive, at 44m (144ft) long. It tells the story of some of Singapore's early immigrants. Yip says it's important to preserve Singapore's heritage, but he'll only work at weekends, while he sticks with his 'proper' job as a full-time accountant!

SKINNY DIPPING

FULLERTON SQUARE, SINGAPORE RIVER

Five boys throw off their clothes and leap into the Singapore River. It looks like a scene that could happen today, but the image is frozen in time, because it's a bronze sculpture, by Chong Fah Cheong. The boys are children of the very fir immigrants to Singapore who, having no toys and absolutely no gadgets to play with, would have us the river as a huge swimming pool and playgroun

SOUNDS OF THE CENTURY

ASIAN CIVILISATIONS MUSEUM, EMPRESS PLACE

Giant stainless steel balls make up an artwork called *24 Hours in Singapore* that children love to race around. Looking into the balls is like looking through a wide-angle lens, and for a while, your reflection is part of the art. Listening carefully, you can pick out recordings of the MRT station, the bus stop, the wet market, the port – all essential sounds of Singapore daily life. Artist Baet Yeok Kuan hopes future generations will enjoy the sounds of the early 21st century, and that children won't stop racing around the mirror balls.

KID STYLE

NATIONAL GALLERY SINGAPORE, ST. ANDREW'S ROAD

The Keppel Centre in Singapore's National Gallery is an art space with a difference. It's aimed at children and families, with exhibits that encourage kids to get creative. They might walk through illustrated forests and past giant sea monsters in their own enormous picture book, or look at a perfect plasticine model of Singapore by a boy aged just 13! Kids can even make a clay pot without getting their hands dirty... because it's all done by computer!

search: FENG SHUI

📍 LOCATION! LOCATION!

Feng shui means 'wind' and 'water'. It's a philosophy that began centuries ago to help people find the best places to live – and the best places to be buried when they died. Feng shui is based around the five elements of Chinese tradition – fire, earth, metal, water and wood – and the shapes, colours and qualities that connect with each element.

4,200 WORKS OF ART IN THE HOTEL'S HALLS

S$5 MILLION (£2.71 MILLION) VALUE OF ART IN THE HOTEL

HAJI LANE

MAKING AN ENTRANCE

THE RITZ-CARLTON, RAFFLES AVENUE

Feng shui was important to the design of the classy Ritz-Carlton. Its entrance is open and spacious, allowing 'wind' to pass through the main doors, while 'water' is present in the mother-of-pearl windowpanes and water feature. The halls of the hotel are filled with works of art, and the huge sculpture hanging from the lobby ceiling represents 'fire'. *Cornucopia*, as it's called, was created by American artist Frank Stella from three tonnes of fibreglass. It's huge, dramatic and powerful, but, surprisingly, Frank's idea was inspired by a sun visor!

THE RITZ-CARLTON

TROLLEY RIDE

HAJI LANE

The punishment for graffiti in Singapore is a severe beating! So it's rare to find street art here. Luckily, Lithuanian-born Ernest Zacharevic was commissioned to paint on these walls. Zacharevic's paintings are full of fun and often use real objects – he's painted characters on street bollards, and these painted shopping trolleys have real-looking passengers. Ernest says he prefers to work with children, because they don't care what they look like and, of course, they love to play.

OT TOPIC

TIONAL MUSEUM OF NGAPORE, STAMFORD ROAD

nari Nahappan became so fascinated chillies that they started to dominate art, and now her sculptures of lies and seeds are dotted across gapore. This one, *Pedas Pedas* aning very spicy), is in the garden he National Museum of Singapore. nari is fascinated by the different pes, colours and sizes chillies come nd buys them wherever she goes. loves the fact that something small can be so powerful any locals would say that gapore is like that, too!

HOLLAND VILLAGE

NATIONAL MUSEUM OF SINGAPORE

ASIAN INFUSION

HOLLAND VILLAGE

Fed up with Singapore fashion being dominated by Western style, Priscilla Shunmugam decided to change things. Born to Chinese and Indian parents, she grew up in Malaysia, studied in London and now lives in Singapore. Her fashion label, Ong Shunmugam, uses her parents' surnames, and the family connection is perfect, because Priscilla's designs are based on traditional Southeast Asian styles and fabrics. She's brought traditional dresses such as the Chinese *cheongsam*, the Japanese *kimono* and the Malaysian *baju kurung* bang up to date and made them available for all women to wear.

GO WILD IN THE CITY

Singapore's wildlife dwindled as the settlements grew, but there's still plenty to see. Tigers may be long gone in the wild here, but luckily you can see them, orangutans and much more at the zoo!

GARDENS OF THE FUTURE

GARDENS BY THE BAY

It's safe to say there are no other gardens in the world quite like these three. Built on reclaimed land, with manmade trees, two space-age greenhouse domes and over one million plants, Gardens by the Bay is probably Singapore's top visitor attraction.

TREEMENDOUS!

Instead of waiting decades for tall trees to grow, Gardens by the Bay built its own from concrete and steel! In total, 18 supertrees sprout from the gardens, and even though they're manmade they're teeming with life. Tropical climbing plants, ferns and epiphytes (plants that grow from other plants instead of soil) cover the trees' metal frames. The trees themselves aren't just for show either: they can generate light from solar energy, act as air vents, collect rainwater and provide shelter down below. At the top of the tallest supertree there's even a restaurant!

EACH TREE IS 25–50M (82–162FT) TALL.

LIGHTS UP AT NIGHT!

STEEL FRAME

...JPERCOOL

...nice and cool inside the Cloud Forest
...e – a welcome relief from Singapore's
...ical heat. Visitors first take a lift to
...top of the mountain 35m (115ft) high
...then look down over the waterfall
...bling from its summit! Meat-eating
...ts such as Venus flytraps lurk at the
...in the Lost World, and as visitors walk
...n through the clouds, they'll see stalactites
...stalagmites in the Crystal Mountain and
...e-dwelling plants in the Secret Garden.

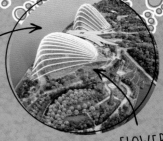

CLOUD
FOREST

FLOWER
DOME

58M
(190FT) HEIGHT OF
THE CLOUD FOREST

23-25°C
(73-77°F) TEMPERATURE
INSIDE THE CLOUD BIOME

AFRICAN BAOBAB TREE

BLOOMING AMAZING

In 2015, the Flower Dome entered the Guinness
World Records as the largest greenhouse in the
world. Inside, nine different gardens display
the plants of five different continents, from
a Mediterranean olive tree that's over 1,000 years
old, to a huge African baobab tree that only flowers
at night and an Australian grass tree that can live
for 600 years! A fabulous flower field in the middle
of the dome changes with the seasons, with every
colour of tulip imaginable in spring and pumpkins
little, large and enormous especially for Halloween.

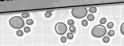
LITTLE AND LARGE

MERLION PARK

With its lion's head and fishy tail, the Merlion statue looks like something from Chinese mythology. In fact, the creature was dreamed up in 1964 for the Singapore Tourism Board! The statue's head represents the lion behind the name of the city (see page 16) and the tail refers to Singapore's origins as a fishing village. The 8.6m (28ft) statue was unveiled in 1972 with a smaller cub close by that's just 2m (6.6ft) tall. The creature quickly caught on, and now there are seven Merlion statues around the city.

OTTER SPOTTING

SINGAPORE RIVER

Smooth-coated otters were presumed extinct in Singapore after numbers dwindled in the 1970s. But, just like the Singapore River, they've made a magnificent comeback. Settling in north Singapore at first, otters have now taken up residence in Marina Bay. Locals love to come otter spotting, and the otters are happy to put on a show: catching fish, frolicking about in the water and rolling around in the riverbank sand. They've even starred in an episode of the David Attenborough documentary series *Wild City*!

70 TONNES
(77 SH TONS) WEIGHT OF LARGER STATUE

3 TONNES
(3.3 SH TONS) WEIGHT OF THE CUB STATUE

17:30
THE BEST TIME OF DAY FOR OTTER SPOTTING

S$80,000
(£44,000) VALUE OF KOI CARP
THAT DISAPPEARED FROM SENTOSA ISLAND
(OTTERS WERE SUSPECTED OF EATING THEM)

DINOSAURS AND MORE

LEE KONG CHIAN NATURAL HISTORY MUSEUM

The three dinosaurs in this museum are 150-million-year-old sauropods nicknamed Prince, Apollonia and Twinky. They may be all one family, with Twinky the baby at just 12m (39ft) long. They're 80 per cent complete and are some of the finest dinosaur skeletons in the world. Surprisingly, two were even found with their skulls intact. But there's lots more to this museum than the dinosaurs. With Southeast Asian natural history divided into 20 zones, visitors can go back in time to find out how the many different forms of life began.

500,000 NUMBER OF PLANT AND ANIMAL SPECIMENS IN THE MUSEUM

LEE KONG CHIAN NATURAL HISTORY MUSEUM

TIGER TERROR

BUKIT MERAH

Tigers once hunted for wild boar and deer in the forests here, and back in 1831, Singapore's very first newspaper reported a tiger attack on a Chinese worker. The man was killed, and, soon after, so was the tiger. As forests were turned into plantations, rewards were offered for shooting tigers dead. In the 1900s, that reward was so high that hunting became a serious business and tiger numbers dwindled. The very last Singapore tiger was shot and killed in the 1930s.

350 NUMBER OF PEOPLE REPORTED KILLED BY TIGERS IN THE 1860s

BUKIT MERAH

CHEEKY MONKEYS

MACRITCHIE RESERVOIR PARK

Long-tailed macaque monkeys are often seen swinging through the trees of this park in troops of up to 30. They eat leaves, shoots, flowers, small reptiles, spiders, insects and over 180 species of plant. With so many foods available, people really don't need to feed the monkeys, but they do and it causes problems. If humans meet a monkey, they're instructed to stay calm and quiet, back away slowly and definitely keep food out of the way!

AH MENG WAS PROBABLY THE WORLD'S MOST FAMOUS ORANGUTAN. CELEBRITIES FLOCKED TO MEET HER, AND AFTER SHE DIED, 4,000 PEOPLE CAME TO HER MEMORIAL SERVICE.

MACAQUES ARE CLEVER CREATURES. THEY USE STONES AS TOOLS TO HELP THEM FORAGE AND THEY'VE EVEN BEEN SPOTTED USING HUMAN HAIR AS DENTAL FLOSS!

ZOOPERSTAR

SINGAPORE ZOO

Asia's number one zoo is an 'open zoo', because it hides the barriers between humans and animals behind waterfalls and leafy vegetation. For years, an orangutan called Ah Meng was the zoo's big star. She'd arrived in the 1970s after being kept illegally as a pet. Visitors ate breakfast with her, came to her birthday parties and she starred in over 30 travel films. She died in 2008 aged 48 – that's roughly 95 in human years – leaving her partner, Charlie, and five children behind her. Now her granddaughter, Ishta, is the zoo's new animal ambassador.

search: MANGROVE WILDLIFE

MUD GLORIOUS MUD

All kinds of creatures hide in the roots and branches of the mangrove. Tree-climbing crabs clamber up the trunks at high tide to hide from predators, giant mudskippers, up to 27cm (11in) long, jump around in the puddles, and sometimes, there's even an estuarine man-eating crocodile lazing around on the riverbank!

FROGOLOGY
JURONG FROG FARM

Large American bullfrogs are reared here for their meat, but visitors are also welcome on the farm to learn about them. Children can feed the frogs, listen to the frog chorus and find out how to tell a male from a female – they might even get a frog to sit on their head! Frog meat is popular in Singapore and it's a healthy option, too, because it's low in fat and high in protein. The Wans, who run the farm, have found plenty of unusual frog recipes, but frog-skin chips is quite probably the strangest!

0.5% THE AMOUNT OF MANGROVE LEFT IN SINGAPORE TODAY

PROPORTION OF SINGAPORE MADE UP OF MANGROVE IN THE 1820s **13%**

ĪRACULOUS MANGROVES
ÜNGEI BULOH

ngrove forests are found in tropical areas on the boundary ween land and water and are rich with biodiversity. One of gapore's last remaining mangrove forests can be found at ngei Buloh. People used to think mangrove trees were useless, their roots protect the coastline and allow fish to thrive. as have changed, and today scientists are realizing that mangrove plant might even help with climate change. an absorb pollution, protect the land from floods, ms and hurricanes and survive in water 100 times tier than most other plants can stand.

JURONG FROG FARM

"Hope I don't croak it today!"

SUNGEI BULOH

UP ALL NIGHT

The Singapore sunset has been and gone by 7:30pm on any night of the year, but the evenings can be a relief after the intense daytime heat. And there's loads to do here after dark...

SPOT THE CREATURE

NIGHT SAFARI

Opened in 1994, this was the world's first night-time zoo. Visitors can stay right through until midnight and, with the help of clever lighting, spot very unusual nocturnal creatures. The fishing cat is twice the size of a house cat, with webbed paws that help it swim to catch its prey; the greater mouse deer is one of the world's smallest hoofed mammals; and the beautiful, big-eyed slow loris (a small primate) has a vicious, poisonous bite. Visitors can travel by tram or even walk along trails, looking at tigers and other animals safely, through glass.

THE RAIL CORRIDOR

STEPPING ON STAR

THE RAIL CORRIDOR, NEAR BUKIT PANJANG MRT STATION

This 24km (15 mile) stretch of old railway line has been set aside as a green corridor so locals can esca from the city. Anyone strolling along one short stret of old track after dark might find that it twinkles like the night sky! That's because it's scattered with strontium aluminate minerals that absorb ultra-violet rays from the sun during the day, so they can light up the path at night. If locals decide they like this idea, the may soon be many more sparkly paths around Singapor

NIGHT SAFARI

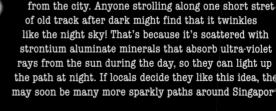

START

ORTH THE WAIT

EYLANG SERAI

ch year, in the month of Ramadan, Muslims
t from sunrise to sunset. But, everything
nges after dark! Crowds head to Ramadan
aars, like this one, to shop for clothes, buy
arpet, maybe get a henna tattoo and definitely
something to eat! It's absolutely worth waiting
some of the delicious dishes on offer here, like
u bamboo – rice flour steamed in hollowed-out
nboo, served with a stick of palm sugar and
ted coconut. Yes please!

DRONING ON

MARINA BAY SANDS HOTEL, BAYFRONT AVENUE

Whiz up to the Observation Deck on the 57th floor of this
hotel and you'll get a fantastic view of the city at night.
It's ideal for watching light shows, too, like the unusual
one that happened after dark on National Day 2017.
Strange lights appeared over the bay – they weren't
shining up from the ground and they weren't fireworks.
Then they flew together to make seven shimmering
shapes, including an arrow, a heart shape, a Merlion,
and even the outline of Singapore. The lights were
carried by computer-controlled drones – new
technology at its finest!

STARS UNDER THE STARS
FORT CANNING GREEN

This is a great place for a picnic at the best of times, but because the green is on a slope it's perfect for watching performances, too. Each year, *Shakespeare in the Park* and *Ballet Under the Stars* offer audiences amazing open-air, after-dark spectacles with stars of theatre and dance. A lucky few can book VIP cushions in the front rows and have a pre-prepared picnic hamper brought to them.

BLINKING BRILLIANT
NATIONAL MUSEUM OF SINGAPORE, STAMFORD ROAD

Over one week in August, there are all sorts of outdoor evening events here featuring artists, acrobats, magicians and even wrestlers. The Night Festival also invites visitors to follow a trail of illuminated buildings and incredible light sculptures. In 2017, artist Karel Bata projected a series of portraits onto a huge tree. As the breeze brushed the leaves and branches, the expressions on the faces seemed to change. He called the work *The Tree that Blinked*. The effect was so surprising that some people thought the artist had painted the tree by hand!

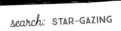

NATIONAL MUSEUM OF SINGAPORE

search: STAR-GAZING

📍 STAGE IN THE SKY

On 27 January 2016, there was no need for performers, because the planets were stars of the show. Eager stargazers laid their blankets on the green just before dawn and saw Mercury, Venus, Mars, Saturn and Jupiter together for the first time in over ten years.

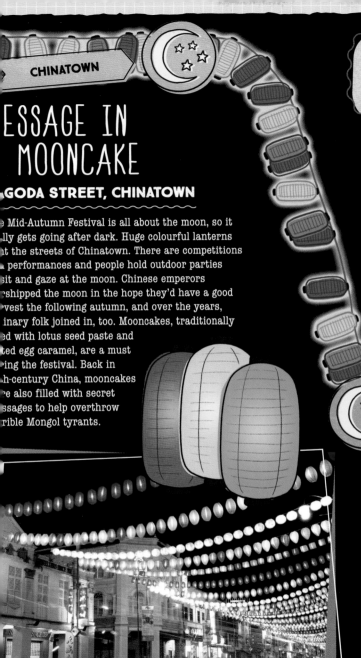

CHINATOWN

ESSAGE IN MOONCAKE

GODA STREET, CHINATOWN

e Mid-Autumn Festival is all about the moon, so it lly gets going after dark. Huge colourful lanterns t the streets of Chinatown. There are competitions performances and people hold outdoor parties sit and gaze at the moon. Chinese emperors rshipped the moon in the hope they'd have a good vest the following autumn, and over the years, inary folk joined in, too. Mooncakes, traditionally ed with lotus seed paste and ted egg caramel, are a must ing the festival. Back in h-century China, mooncakes e also filled with secret ssages to help overthrow rible Mongol tyrants.

A NIGHTTIME GRAND PRIX (SEE PAGE 14) IS DEFINITELY THE BEST OPTION FOR RACING DRIVERS — IT'S SO HOT AND HUMID IN SINGAPORE! AN EVENING START TIME ALSO MEANS THAT EUROPEAN FANS CAN WATCH THE RACE IN THE AFTERNOON.

SENTOSA

RUNNING IN THE DARK

THE COLOR RUN, SENTOSA

Whole families come out dressed in blinding neon gear to run this crazy 5km (3 mile) race. In September 2017, Singapore hosted its first-ever Color Run at night – it's cooler after dark, so it's also easier to run! The race pack included a special blacklight headlamp that picks up the glow around the track. Along the route, runners were blasted with coloured powder, luminous bubbles and glowing neon foam. Finish times didn't matter, and walking was fine, because this race was all about having fun, which is why it ended with a massive party!

INDEX

INDEX

FURTHER READING

Make My Day Singapore
Lonely Planet

Aimed at adults, this guide is great for planning family trips around Singapore. It offers suggestions for morning, afternoon and evening activities to ensure you make the most out of your visit.

Singapore Cooking
by Terry Tan and Christopher Tan

This recipe book, aimed at adults, can be used to cook a range of Singaporean dishes with kids. It has lots of colourful photos and sections on the basic ingredients that are used for many dishes.

The Cities Book
Lonely Planet

Find out what it's like to grow up in Singapore and many of the world's other great cities. Covering festivals, history, architecture and more this book gives you the insider's view of Singapore so you know what it's really like to live there.

Find and Seek Singapore
by Sally Roydhouse

A journey through Singapore seen through the eyes of a child, this picture book combines rhyme with illustration to conjure up a unique view of the city.

Mudley Explores Singapore: An Amazing Adventure into the Lion City
by Arp Raph Broadhead

Mudley belongs to Sophia, who always makes sure her cuddly bear is packed into her daddy's suitcase when he goes abroad to work. Join Mudley the bear on his travels in Singapore in this book.

Lion City Adventures
by Don Bosco

Aimed at older kids, this guide has interactive activities that take you all over Singapore. It presents the city in short informative sections on language, culture and history.